The Missing Link

Teaching and Learning Critical Success Skills

Steve Heisler

ROWMAN & LITTLEFIELD EDUCATION
A division of
ROWMAN & LITTLEFIELD
Lanham • Boulder • New York • Toronto • Plymouth, UK

Published by Rowman & Littlefield Education
A division of Rowman & Littlefield
4501 Forbes Boulevard, Suite 200, Lanham, Maryland 20706
www.rowman.com

10 Thornbury Road, Plymouth PL6 7PP, United Kingdom

Copyright © 2014 by Steve Heisler

All rights reserved. No part of this book may be reproduced in any form or by any electronic or mechanical means, including information storage and retrieval systems, without written permission from the publisher, except by a reviewer who may quote passages in a review.

British Library Cataloguing in Publication Information Available

Library of Congress Cataloging-in-Publication Data

Heisler, Steve.
The missing link : teaching and learning critical success skills / Steve Heisler.
pages cm.
Includes bibliographical references and index.
ISBN 978-1-61048-965-2 (cloth) — ISBN 978-1-61048-966-9 (pbk.) — ISBN 978-1-61048-967-6 (ebook)
1. Critical thinking—Study and teaching. 2. Learning strategies. 3. Achievement motivation. 4. Success. 5. Life skills. I. Title.
LB1590.3.H46 2014
370.15'2—dc23
2013049959

Contents

Acknowledgments		vii
Preface		ix
Introduction		xiii
1	What It Is, and What It Ain't	1
2	Three Keys: Facilitate, Engage, Communicate	7
3	Either We Act as a Family, or Forget It	15
4	Buying In Is the Easy Part	29
5	A Simple Prescription for Self-Regulation and Decision-Making: Take These Frequently, Every Day	45
6	Exercises and Outcomes I: Skills	77
7	Exercises and Outcomes II: Application	105
Afterword: What Matters Tomorrow Is Tomorrow: Closing Thoughts		125

Acknowledgments

I am indebted to many people; it is impossible to thank all those who have influenced me or contributed to this book directly and indirectly. "I want to thank everyone I ever met in my whole life," said Maureen Stapelton, winning her Academy Award. That's how I feel as well.

I am grateful to Tom Koerner and Caitlin Crawford of R&L Publishing Group for seeing value in my book and for shepherding it through the publication process. I am also very thankful for the legal and negotiating support of my friend Mark Diller.

Special thanks to my sister, Cynthia Heisler Wishkovky, and her husband, Adam, for many kindnesses, love, and support over the years and for the courage they have always shown in the face of multiple struggles. I am especially indebted to them for my two nephews, Joel and Ariel, whose growth and continued successes have been so instructive and mean so much to me.

I am grateful to my students over the years. This book is essentially an amalgam of what I have learned from all of them. I am also deeply grateful to have had the opportunity to work for Carol Lefelt, a brilliant teacher and supervisor, whose compassionate, wise leadership and friendship has helped me become a better teacher and a better person. I am particularly thankful for all the work she did in helping make this manuscript more cogent and readable.

I am most deeply indebted to my amazing son, Ben Heisler, and my extraordinary wife, Karen Kanter, an exceptionally fine teacher herself. Many of the ideas that evolved into this book came directly from them, as has so much of what I have learned about hope and compassion and success and courage and laughter and love. Even if I could actually find the words to express how deeply they are integral to my very existence and how deeply they are both loved, it would be so elemental it would just come out as breath anyway. Every word of this book is dedicated to them both, and to the memory of my parents, Jack and Sylvia Heisler.

Preface

The world-famous experiment that defined one of the key ingredients for student success happened more than forty-five years ago. In this experiment, Walter Mischel, a professor of psychology at Stamford, tested several hundred preschoolers' ability to delay gratification. These students were brought, one at a time, into a room with a chair, a table, a wall clock, and a plate of candy.

They were told that they could have one piece of candy: however, they were also told that if they waited before eating that piece of candy until the tester returned to the room, they could have a second piece of candy. Not surprisingly, fewer than 30 percent of these children were able to wait even five minutes in order to get the second piece of candy. Thirty percent. Not a shock.

What was shocking though was Mischel's discovery of the clear correlation between school success and this ability to delay gratification. Those students who showed greater proclivity to self-regulation were exactly the same students who, Mischel later discovered, consistently led their classes academically, scored hundreds of points higher on their SATs, and generally attended the top-ranked universities.

The genesis of this book is rooted in a single moment decades ago when one of my elderly neighbors buttonholed me in my lobby of my apartment building and disgorged, in the space of about six minutes, every regret he had ever had. He identified, in particular, his regret at having lost the only woman he ever loved. And he lost her simply because she got tired of waiting for him to make up his mind about marrying her.

"Yeah, well, that's how it is. Bing, bang, boom, your life goes by. So here I am, alone. Anyway, what I'm going to do is I'm going to take the bus down to South Ferry, maybe take the ferry to Staten Island and then the bus back home."

"Subway's quicker," I suggested.

"Yeah, I know, but the bus kills more time. You know what I mean? It kills more time."

In a moment of terror I thought: is this old man the me that I am moving toward becoming? I was in a moribund state at that time, unable to do the writing I wanted to do, and in the waning days of a fruitless acting career that was morphing into a restaurant career I did not want. In a moment of fear frozen in time I wondered: was I moving along in my life, or merely moving through my days? Much like the narrator in Robert Frost's poem "The Road Not Taken," a poem that can be used to teach decision-making, I had also come to a crossroads.

Understanding that people can see poetry in wildly different ways, Frost's poem appears to be both a metaphor about life as well as a poem expressing a moment of decision-making. At a point of divergence the narrator decides to continue on the road less traveled because it calls to him as having the "better claim/because it was grassy and wanted wear." The speaker defines himself with this choice, but once made, the "action" of the poem essentially ends and the tense shifts from present to future: "I shall be telling this, somewhere, ages and ages hence, with a sigh." The speaker knows that his decision will make "all the difference," but whether it will be positive or a negative will be left to the vagaries of future turnings.

When my brain started working again, I vowed to not let my life happen to me: I would take control, though I had little idea at the time about how. All I knew was that, somehow, from that moment forward I would always be able to say about my life, from whatever swank or shabby perspective I might be viewing it, that I planned it, that I made the choices, and that I was responsible for it. If decades hence an old, impoverished me met a young actor in that same crappy lobby, at least I could say that my bing, bang, boom life *didn't* just go by. At least the choice of how I lived it was mine, and I made the choice to live it the way I wanted every day.

Though this is where my understanding of success skills is rooted, it was only later, after I had shifted into education, that I began to get an understanding of what happened in that moment, and the importance of what I had begun to learn as a result of it. As a young alternate-route teacher in a New York City high school, and later at a middle/high school in New Jersey, with little in the way of formal pedagogical training and my own less-than-stellar early academic career my only real teaching laboratory, I guess that I was freer than most to think differently about students and school.

I sensed, without really understanding, Mischel's finding that most of the students who performed well in school, and who were often enrolled in AP and honors classes, were not actually a whole lot "smarter" than the students who underperformed or were enrolled in what the students themselves, sadly, called the "Bobo" classes.

To be sure, our accelerated students (I had then and continue to have a real bias against calling these classes an "honor") were more learned, better skilled, and more capable than many of my students in the less-accelerated classes. Initially, truth be told, I also bought into what Dr. Robert Brooks calls the "fallacy of laziness." However, I soon realized that most of the students' skills and learning seemed largely a function of what we referred to back then as work ethic rather than innate ability.

Much of the talk in teachers' lounges then, if there was talk at all about teaching, centered mainly on what kids were not doing, and what parents were not doing to help their kids. While I saw that all of this was essentially true, I also saw students' lack of work ethic as an impediment not only to their success but to my success as well.

I had come to teaching after having invested, in the time since my hallway meeting, more than a dozen years in the self-driven struggle to write several novels. I had evolved from a "lazy kid," who spent most of his adolescent summers in school remediating failed classes, to a highly disciplined writer who wrote for hours every day and worked nights to support himself. Not only was I results oriented, but also because of my total control over my writing (alas, only the writing but not the publishing portion), I believed that I had some power over my students as well.

This was fortunate because by the time I realized I had only a bit of influence (and very little power) over my students, I had already begun evolving strategies that essentially helped influence and empower my students to take control of their education and lives.

It does work. An example I often look to—it is what I have often referred to as being one of the true highlights of my professional life—happened one late afternoon several years ago. One of my students from a high school in New York City called me at home a few years after he had graduated. This was well before cellular phones became affordable to teachers and the advent of social networking.

"Mr. H?" he said. "I was thinking about you the other day, about something that you taught us like *all* the time, about decision-making. You know, I used to be a little annoyed, your talking about it so much but I gotta say, man, it really came in handy.

"You know Mr. H, my grades are really good, I'm in a fraternity, and I have plenty of time to do my work and play around. Mr. H, *I am having a great time in college*. But something came up recently. One of my professors asked me to be a part of a research project, for like no money, and he said that I would have to put in like twenty or thirty hours a week.

"I gotta be honest . . . thirty hours a week on a research project is just about the last thing that I wanted to do—did I mention I am having a great time at college? Those hours a week are all going to come out of my play time! I gotta be real: my first instinct was to say, 'Forget it.'

"But then I remembered about all those discussions, looking ahead to make a decision today; I even remember the words you used: *vision, initiative,* and *perspective*. I know I want to go to graduate school and earn a psych doctorate. I know that being a part of this research project will give me publication credentials, as well as practical experience. I know that if I keep my grades up and add stuff like this to my application, it's going to make getting into the grad school I want to go to that much easier. And then I knew what I needed to do, and it was easy—it was maybe the easiest decision I ever made in my life. I'm going to join the research project, and I just wanted to call and thank you."

The ideas and procedures that eventually evolved into this book were born from just such belief in the power of teaching to transform, and in the belief that every single child in the world wants to be successful. The problem is, if they can't be successful at being successful, they'll be successful at screwing up. This book is an attempt to help change the latter to the former.

Introduction

When I began writing this book several months ago I went back and forth about whether this was a book for parents, kids, or professional teachers, and while I think the information in this book may embrace the needs of such different reading audiences, ultimately I chose to address, primarily, professional educators and relationships in schools.

The use of the term *professional educator* (meant to include teachers, administrators, and school support personnel) is purposeful because, in reality, there are teachers everywhere. Virtually anyone, anywhere, at any time, for good or ill, can be the catalyst for a meaningful and memorable learning experience. This designation of professionalism is not to denigrate a single one of these moments happened upon by parents, siblings, neighbors, coworkers, store clerks, police officers, coaches, spouses, cab drivers, and even our children.

Indeed anyone, at any time, anywhere can be a teacher. We wear our teaching moments as badges of honor, medals of our own importance, and they should be. People who teach us (though not necessarily all of those through whom we learn) ought to be honored to a greater degree than they usually are. Moreover, in the panoply of learning experiences that we accrue in our lives, probably only a very small fraction of them actually occur in school.

The ideas in this book apply to those teaching moments as well as the teaching moments fostered by professional educators. However, while anyone might happen on a teachable moment and respond appropriately, professional educators are people who create these teachable moments intentionally, rather than by accident, and then take advantage of them by actually using those moments to make sure students learn. That is the difference.

A professional teacher, like most highly skilled professionals, is prepared, practiced, and perceptive and is capable of responding intentionally to ever-changing inputs with a dogged focus on specific, meaningful, student-centered outcomes. However, even for the most professional professionals, complexities arise that make success if not impossible, very difficult. The best batters in baseball miss more times than they hit. This may be true for teachers, too.

It is not necessarily in the nature of our job to fail, but it is definitely a reality of our work. I have tried not to forget that through my own shortcomings, professionally and personally, I was not able to be the right teacher for any number of students more frequently than I would ever care to admit. However, it is equally a part of our professional standards to try to reset the clock—to continue to learn, to think again, to plan again, and mostly, not only to try again but also to create the desire and the opportunities for our students to keep on trying.

An important purpose of this book is about being able to teach our children and our students, as best we can, to do just that: keep on trying. This book proposes to help professional educators and others understand how to teach students:

- skills that, habitually applied, may enhance students' ability to be successful in school and in life.
- to continue to apply these success skills relentlessly all throughout their lives.
- to become sharply aware of the huge number of things that are within their control.
- to become sharply aware of the huge number of things that are not in their control.
- to wrap their minds and hearts around the idea that what they choose is who they become.

However, while understanding is critical, the main intention is to show already-overloaded professional educators how using and teaching these skills can be infused in simple, effective ways into already-existing schoolwork and curriculum in about the same time frame. However, in order to teach students to infuse critical success skills into their everyday lives and learning, teachers must value process itself, and at the same time understand the difficulty of process. Because of that it is even more important to teach these skills within a cooperative, consistent, clinical, and even familylike whole-school milieu using common language and practices. Although many teachers and administrators understand the importance of consistency of content and process when it comes to academics, fewer seem to understand the necessity of a like process when it comes to changing behaviors and changing hearts.

This book is structured around the idea that identifying goals and visions for our future, and actually moving positively in the direction of them, is all about managing the process. It is particularly true if, in order to approach achieving that vision, behavioral or emotional or self-perceptual change has to occur. There are few circumstances under such demanding conditions where there aren't some significant challenges that must be met.

Being supported through the ups and downs of achievement, and of building a belief in one's capacity to succeed—so that our children can maintain hope and positivity through such a process—is critical. It is not too strong to say that without hope, without belief, little that isn't gotten immediately is ever gotten at all. While seeing this kind of personal developmental learning as being the responsibility of the school may be an arguable proposition, that such hope and belief is a core practice of the successful student is not. That being the case, if it isn't learned outside of school, then it certainly seems to fall to the school to have to teach it.

The arrangement of this book moves from the theoretical to the practical for just this reason. Much is introduced in the first few chapters (gone into greater detail later on) that identifies the rationale for instituting a structure such as a "professional family." It brings into the conversation the means by which we can behave and interact so that we are fostering student will and student empowerment, and looking at the development of the individual long term. The power of the positive support of compassionate and empathic adults is incalculable in supporting the difficult work of change, which at its base is believing in the process itself. It is a difficult road at any age, let alone as a youth, to design and work toward an unguaranteed future to which one can be committed over a long period of time.

While suggestions are offered in respect of how to teach these specific skills (such as self-regulation and time management), the main focus is on individual and communal professional behaviors and structures designed to promote a unified approach to learning these skills. In addition to the suggestions for direct teaching included here, there is an enormous amount of information and suggestions available in publications and on the internet that offer a plethora of activities to develop self-regulation, organization, pro-social behavior, and so forth. In this book it is only chapter 5 that actually details the core decision-making skill in which students will need to become proficient, and it is bookended by the theories spoken of earlier and the practices that adults must engage in to help students develop proficiency.

At least at the outset it is critical to understand that any positive actions a student undertakes are somewhat less important than the fact that he or she is engaging in positive actions. We need to focus on how, over a school day or a school year or a school lifetime, we can promote a single message of expectation and support, how we can help students learn how to work those actions into achievement outcomes, through multiple setbacks and over long periods of time, not because we want them to but because they value it, because it makes sense, and because it works for their lives. Even while this text will certainly not be *the* answer, I am hopeful that it might at least move the conversation along toward recreating school as just such a collaborative, familial environment that sees its mission as helping students learn how to help themselves.

ONE
What It Is, and What It Ain't

> The difficulty of success is to be able to give up what you are today for the hope of what you might become tomorrow. —Anonymous

THE PROCESS *IS* THE PRODUCT

A great impediment to most programs that have offered assistance to teachers, administrators, parents, and schools has generally been the idea that whatever the problem is, this program will fix it. Our all-too-human hope that kids can be "cured" of what ails them, and that those programs can be injected into their veins like a medication, has proven only to be a whet for our own self-delusion.

It is certainly not wrong, on occasion, to buy a lottery ticket with the vague hope that one single lightning strike (the odds are actually more in your favor that you will be struck by lightning rather than win a lottery) will assuage our financial cares so that we'll be able to spend our waning years sipping piña coladas on the porch of a beach house watching ocean waves, glitteringly irradiated, gently lap the white sands of the beach.

It's great to dream big but not if the dream of the big win keeps us from making progress. Buy the ticket, absolutely, but also lay aside a few bucks so, perhaps, one day, you can afford to pay the neighbor kid a few bucks to shovel the snow on your walk instead of breaking your back out there yourself.

What must be stated, unequivocally, is that this process of teaching critical success skills is not an injection. Teaching students what critical success skills are, and even how to apply them, will, for the most part, not fix a thing. In fact it seems fairly clear that teaching these skills as directives and information alone has little long-term effect.

That is not to say that just making the importance of these skills known has no value. Most dedicated teachers will acknowledge that to merely raise awareness, to put anything positive into the mind of a student is never wasted. However, the key in teaching critical success skills is that there has to be a commitment to process, and often a long process, wherein these skills are identified, practiced, consciously applied, and then finally internalized and applied with some automaticity.

Essentially, when it comes to teaching students critical success skills, *the process is the product.* Those persons seeking a quick fix for the issues facing their children and their students would probably be better served by searching elsewhere.

Recently success skills were introduced to some teachers and several classes of disaffected students in a very low-performing New York City high school. The kids were very engaged, and even some teachers, who were not otherwise absorbed in reading newspapers or their computers, also expressed excitement. They were learning how some of their own behaviors might have been keeping them from achieving their own goals, and how they might go about changing their approach to goal setting and long-term planning to increase achievement.

Indeed, in classes where students are normally out the door before the bell has stopped ringing, several students milled around to discuss success skills further. And even several days later a student gushed how learning about these skills in that presentation had a powerful impact on him. Jose (not his real name) said that the ideas really caught his attention.

"Man," he said, "I just realized, as you were talking, you were talking right to me. I have just been screwing myself over. You know, I have been to school every day this week. That's like the first time I have been to school every day since grade school!"

Of course this is a great moment, but it is only a beginning—a great beginning, to be sure, but only a beginning. To help students really apply these skills in a meaningful way that promotes personal change, students must understand that a step in the right direction is, after all, just a step in the right direction. It must be followed, purposefully, by many more such steps.

The infrastructure to this entire idea is *continuous facilitative guidance.* (Along with the other elements discussed in these opening chapters, this element will be addressed with greater depth throughout the text.) Follow-up facilitation can take many forms from discussion to progress tracking, but it is what is necessary to help a student like Jose stay the course in the times ahead, and to overcome the *power of now*, when frustration allows temptation to have its moment. What Jose needs to learn is what takes the time and the practice: how to say no to something *really good* today to gain a greater reward with something better further along.

For many reasons, Jose was unable to get this kind of guidance, or perhaps Jose was just not sufficiently motivated by a "vision" to allow himself to do this. In not too long a time, Jose started to slide back into old class-cutting behaviors.

This is not a shock because, as was stated earlier, merely knowing is not enough. Jose could only go so far in his desire to change because, in reality, almost nothing that a single person might say can change a person's habits. And habits, ladies and gentlemen, not the words that we speak or the intentions that we have, habits are what is really, fundamentally important.

FIRST WE MAKE OUR HABITS, AND THEN OUR HABITS MAKE US

Habits are neither forged nor changed instantly. Some data out there suggests it takes a certain number of days to create or to change a habit, but however long it takes to form a habit, it seems generally agreed on that, once forged, it's yours forever, for good or ill.

It might be that once your habit has been imprinted you can never really rid yourself it entirely. It appears that remnants of old habits seem to hang on long after that main function of the habit has been altered. Indeed, exchanging a poorer habit for a better one can usually only be achieved through a conscious act of will.

So in changing a habit you actually must first change your consciousness of what you are trying to change and choose to redirect the impulse toward something more positive. Sometimes this is referred to as creating a replacement behavior, which is a very positive approach, but it is just one of several possibilities.

In a recent interview in *Rolling Stone*, Bruce Springsteen described a metaphor that helps him understand life. This defines the process of trying to develop new habits as well. Springsteen said, imagine you are in a car, "and your new selves can't get in, but your old selves can't get out. You can bring new vision and guidance into your life, but you can't lose or forget who you've been and what you've seen." Habit, once formed, is one of the selves in the car.

An apt example concerns a person who was a heavy smoker for twenty years. Though he enjoyed smoking, he tried to quit several times only because he feared the consequences. Yet each time, sometimes even after having stopped for months, he always found an excuse to start again. Increasingly fearful about the consequences, he made a commitment to quit within the year and was confronted by serious anxiety and doom at the consequences of making yet another attempt. And while he did despair, he also hit on an idea. He realized that he did not have to quit at all. All he had to do was simply not light the next cigarette.

A trick of the mind? Perhaps, but the reality was while not smoking forever was overwhelming, simply not lighting the next cigarette seemed doable. If he could just not light the next cigarette, quitting forever would take care of itself. Not to say that was easy, but it helped, at least on some level, to understand that while the misery of quitting was short term, emphysema and lung cancer were forever!

He talked to himself, reasoned with himself, sometimes even aloud, repeating an almost mantra-like set of words: "I am a cigarette addict. I wasn't born liking cigarettes. My first cigarettes made me sick to my stomach yet I willed myself to like them. I trained my body to accept the toxicity of cigarettes and so I am trying to teach my body to unlike them. I may never do this but am deeply committed to just not lighting that next cigarette. All I have to do is hang in for just another minute."

The first day was tough, the next few tougher still, but he hung in, essentially applying his mantra as facilitative guidance, reminding himself to stay focused on his short-term goal, the one he could handle: *just don't light that next cigarette!* He managed some extremely hard moments, and some really hard days, and had to apply lots of strenuous self-management: *just don't light that next cigarette!* He got through a week, then a month: *just don't light that next cigarette!* A month became months, which eventually became years, and the power of the desire to smoke began to wane, making not lighting that next smoke easier and easier. The urges, powerful once, had diminished, but they never went away entirely.

Because smoking had been ingrained into his habitual nature, it will always be "in the car." But because not smoking became as powerful a habit as smoking once was, it became simply easier to manage the urge to smoke. When it arises, that gripping power that wanted its cigarette, *and wanted it now*, has been tamed by the power of the habit to not smoke.

This is an especially important issue approaching changing a student's habit of failure. It is important to remember that you cannot negate negative habits with punishment; even the "punishment" of cancer or emphysema doesn't get all smokers to quit. The impulse that has learned to feed on negative behaviors must be fed and will not tolerate starvation long. But it can be tamed to live on a taste instead of a feast. Eventually a taste as tiny as a thought will satisfy while the driving need can learn to feast on a better, more positive meal.

The critical success skills approach seeks to modify behavioral habits that lead to failure and frustration and in their stead create success habits that lead students to greater self-efficacy, greater personal empowerment, and greater control over the short- and long-term choices they make in their lives. The truth is most students will agree to a positive change (such as agreeing to do homework, or reading) to please the teacher (or parent), or just to get that person off his or her back. However, any teacher who has been in the classroom for more than a moment understands that this kind of meaningful change may begin with compliance but only happens as a result of true desire for change on the part of the student.

But real change demands a belief system that takes the student's desire for change outside of the purview of others. Therefore, facilitating the conversation where students can comfortably be open about deeper fears and goals involves a different level of careful listening and nonthreatening interaction than is usually offered. It also takes serious time to build trust and to express real, genuine compassion for the kid. This is especially true with older students.

There is no question that the earlier you form habits, the easier they are to form and the easier sustaining these habits ends up being. That the young are more impressionable is not news. A good example of building positive habits in the young is the *Tools of the Mind* program, which will be explored with greater depth later in this book.

Tools of the Mind, which calls itself a *Vygotskian* approach to teaching, helps children as young as four form good habits of mind as well as good habits of behavior. Through game playing and even through rudimentary "long term" planning, students begin to develop an ability to pause, reflect, and make decisions in the short term by understanding the effect of those decisions on longer-term plans and goals.

The traditional preschool and kindergarten classroom sometimes takes a less-nuanced approach to forming behavioral habits. Compliance to teacher authority, taught as important in and of itself, is the more accepted means of student training. Most educators rightly agree that school readiness habits, such as compliance to authority, are critically important to foster learning and maintain functional classrooms.

However, compliance alone, without developing good habits of mind, is too often a short-term gain. Compare this to the Tools of the Mind program, which also teaches compliance to authority, but it is taught as a decision that students need to make because such decisions are in the best interest of their own long-term success.

Self-regulation, persistence, resilience, long- and short-term planning, managing personal relationships, and other critical success skills are habits that limn the stories of virtually every successful person. When these behaviors are understood to be integral to success, choosing compliance, for example, over resistance becomes a strength-based rather than a weakness-based choice. It becomes a purposeful means to achieve success rather than a means to avoid somebody's punishment. Compliance alone will not help develop that independent, life-long learner so often identified as the penultimate goal of most school mission statements.

So, while teaching students critical skills offers teachers an opportunity to create deep and lasting change for students, it probably is not going to solve behavioral problems with such ease as may be offered on those TV commercials that promise to give parents an immediate upper hand in their children's inappropriate behavior.

While some of the promises made by these programs may be truthful, both historical and current data from teachers, parents, and administrators tend to underscore the idea that there never really are quick fixes to problem behavior. Like good health, the best approach is to engender good habits before poor habits create significant and sometimes incurable problems.

A powerful and telling statistic reveals that about 80 percent of all suspension time is meted out to the same 10 percent of the students. In other words, the very consequence that is supposed to keep students from misbehaving may well only be working on those students that need such threats the least: those students who can already, at least to some extent, exert some self-control over their behavior. These kinds of statistics are repeated year after year in schools and then, not surprisingly, again in our prison system.

This supposed great deterrent, suspension for students and prison for adults, is, in the end, not a strong enough deterrent for all. Yet judges keep sending the same scofflaws to prison over and over and school administrators keep suspending the same students over and over again. Some do so because they believe, ultimately, it will work (*it's just a question of time!*), some because it is simply easier to get rid of a problem than to deal with it, but most because they simply do not have any other alternative. What this program aspires to be is an alternative.

The core belief on which this book is founded, and its ultimate objective, is that the reader will come to believe that at any age there is hope for change, but never more so than when a person is a student and open still to learning. But hope without a plan is just a dream, and from dreams we always awake.

Teaching students critical success skills is a plan, and one that can work, slowly but effectively, as part of an effective package of teaching and administrative practices to take hope forward into action, behavioral change, and more positive outcomes for many students. And while this program cannot promise any students that their dreams will come true, what it does promise is that taking greater conscious control over the decisions that affect one's future will almost always lead to more positive, more satisfying outcomes.

When a student takes control, when anyone takes control over their decisions, you live, as Thoreau said, deliberately. In the end, isn't that what we always want for ourselves and our children: the right to choose, the wisdom to choose, and to be responsible for ourselves? Given that, once we infuse our children with these aforementioned three things, we have nothing left to do but release our children into the world they will create, and let the chips fall where they may.

TWO

Three Keys

Facilitate, Engage, Communicate

> The best way to give advice to a child is to find out what he wants to do, and then tell him to do it. —Mark Twain

Let's face it: as a group teachers are simply too directive. Teachers have perceptions, judgments, ideas, knowledge, all of which has been honestly come by through meaningful, true experiences, or at least what we imagine are our true experiences. However well meaning, teachers are dying to shape the lives of their young charges by imparting to them opinions of what they should be, and how they should go about being it. It is well meaning, to be sure, but, unfortunately, it is self-serving and probably, to be perfectly frank, bunk. All of this was made clear with the discovery of *Steve Heisler's Theory of Attenuated Relationships*.

This *amazing* theory was born in a crystalline revelation a number of years ago when it came to Heisler's attention that several teachers were relentlessly extolling the extraordinary virtues they displayed when they were students. If they were to be believed, not a single one of them had gotten anything less than an A+ in any of their classes, they never had to be upbraided because of their behavior, they were never anything less than stellar in the classroom, they showed up on time for every single day of school, with their shoes shined, and they had all gotten perfect scores on their SATs. In reality many of these teachers were bright and capable, and several surely did quite well in school, some perhaps even were close to perfect.

However, this crystalline revelation appeared when a student, an exceptionally bright young man who has since gone on to a very distinguished academic career, was noted in the morning announcements for having scored 1580 on his SATs (when 1600 was the highest score). Two teachers even made a point of seeking him out to congratulate him as well as to note that his brilliance was only eclipsed by their own.

"Did you know," the student asked, "that [these two teachers] both got 1600s? That's really amazing."

While there is no hard data on what scores these two teachers might have gotten on their SATs, at least one of them was probably incapable of figuring out how to exit a closet, let alone achieve SAT perfection. The other was so ridiculously competitive that once, at a faculty luncheon, in response to a teacher who made a positive comment about her new air conditioner, began bragging about great the central A/C was in her house.

"I'm actually not a big fan of our central A/C," a third teacher said. "I usually don't mind being warm. I probably only turned it on five or six times last year."

"Well," said the competitive teacher, "I only turned my A/C on twice."

It was in that moment that the theory was born.

Simply put, Steve Heisler's Theory of Attenuated Relationships posits: the further you are away from something you used to do, the more brilliant you used to be at it when you used to do it.

As teachers forget their struggles as students, they begin to believe that back then they were indeed perfect little ladies and gentlemen, *and brilliant*. Likewise, many administrators similarly forget any struggle they had in their classrooms. Listen to some administrators discuss how simply they would have overcome the problems their teachers face and you would think that not only did every single student in every administrator's class go to an Ivy League college on a full scholarship, but also any student who happened by an open door while they were teaching also took the express train to Harvard.

"Memories are like jewels," said Salvador Dali. "The more sparkling they are, the more likely it is that they are false."

Forgetting, however, makes us less effective at understanding, truly understanding, the students in our charge. It leaves us less capable of really helping them. In remembering the real truth of a struggle, what really happened is held to the light rather than that sparkling jewel, and true compassion for others begins.

The following is a brief introduction to the three key behaviors that school and classroom leaders need to exemplify and employ constantly and consistently. The three keys are: *facilitation, engagement,* and *communication*. But underlying these keys, and virtually everything else about effectively teaching success skills, is a belief that in order to make these keys effective, teachers must be truly willing to be empathic and compassionate. These three keys, and the concept of empathic teaching, will be revisited multiple times throughout this book.

1. FACILITATE!

Facilitation is absolutely critical. In fact, the single most important element of this program is a deep and unyielding commitment to facilitation. Without it, the program is a joke.

Genuine compassion is one of the key skills that augment the ability to facilitate. The poet John O'Donohue described it as "the ability to step outside our own perspective, limitation and ego and become attentive in a vulnerable, encouraging, critical and creative way with the hidden world of another person."

Similarly, facilitation is the ability to be present in the internal dialogue of another in an encouraging, critical, and creative way. Teachers' and parents' desire to fix things, in ways that are too often limited by the experiences of their own lives, complicates this. To be facilitative you must be willing to set aside your own beliefs in what should be or ought to be in order to *coach* someone into following his or her own thoughts to where he or she finds the "right" for them.

It's a tall order, to be sure. Consider this.

You are a school baseball coach and you suddenly need another pitcher on your team. How do you go about selecting one? Chances are that what you will not do is just pick whoever it is that happens to be standing nearby. In all likelihood you'll look first for someone who has an interest, or even a facility, for pitching that the athlete himself or herself may not yet have realized. It almost goes without saying that as a coach you would never just select someone, stick them on the mound, and force them to throw.

Indeed, the whole concept is ludicrous. The core of any coaching relationship is built on at least a whisper of willingness that is the foundation of the relationship between the coach and the player. Great coaches leverage the athlete's natural athleticism to improve on existing skills or try to build skills by employing the athlete's desire to excel.

Albert Einstein noted, "Everybody is a genius. But if you judge a fish by its ability to climb a tree, it will live its whole life believing that it is stupid." In this same way, coaching is built out of a trusting relationship grounded in an ability to communicate that defers to the needs of the person being coached rather than the coach's beliefs and needs.

This is the essence of facilitation. Attentive, active listening and the ability to mirror what is being said back to the speaker in a way that allows the speaker to really hear himself or herself are skills that facilitative teachers need to hone. Critically, it is also being absolute in sublimating the desire to be overtly directive, to tell kids what they *ought* to know and do.

There's a great story about a young pitcher who was, by all accounts, pretty mediocre. Now normally a pitcher in baseball will throw "over the top," meaning that he throws in an overhand motion. This young pitcher, however, had a great deal of trouble maintaining such a throwing motion. While many coaches insisted he'd improve by perfecting the more accepted approach, he made little progress from that angle.

One coach, however, rather than trying to fit this young man into the mold of most pitchers, recognized a different natural tendency and facilitated the exact opposite of the other coaches: he helped this young man perfect his natural "submarine" or down-under motion.

Although rare, this "submarine" style has been employed by several pretty great players to major league, even Hall of Fame, results. It is rare because, at least in part, it is rarely encouraged. It's not what a pitcher is "supposed to look like," and few coaches probably understand it as well as they understand the more accepted overhand motion. In this story, the coach didn't know much about the style either but he saw a spark of determination and willingness in this player and together they figured out how to make it work.

Chad Bradford, the young man in this story, was coached in high school by William "Moose" Perry (Moose may well be the all-time greatest nickname, by the way). Bradford wound up pitching in the major leagues, and while his career was hardly distinguished, he did have some standout moments, including a twenty-four-game postseason ERA of 0.39, which is, for those of you not schooled in baseball's statistical parlance, a very, very impressive number.

2. ENGAGE!

All kids want to be successful—it's that simple. Every kid on the planet wants to be successful, and when they grow up, they still want to be successful. Knowing that, it becomes much easier to see what is really true about kids. That is, if they can't be successful at being successful, they'll be successful at screwing up, and many will be successful at it. The very core of building student success skills is the facilitative component that can move a child from screwing up to success, but be warned: facilitation is a complex and involving activity. Much of what passes for facilitation is little more than firing off a few suggestions about what you think someone ought to do.

One assistant principal genuinely thought that when she told a student to "make better choices" as she was meting out a suspension, she was actually accomplishing something. She actually thought highly of it. "I told him," she said, voice dripping with pride, "I told him just like that: you need to make better choices! He heard me—you can bet on that."

Maybe she was making a difference; some people only need simple warnings, or just a bit of information. Some are simply ready to move in the "right" direction and need only a little nudge. There is absolutely no doubt that when you teach in a certain style, and a student enrolled in your class learns in the same style, sparks illuminate both relationships.

But the reality is that most students stay on the path they started on: those who start getting into trouble seem to consistently get into more trouble. They continue to perform at a level below their academic capabilities, continue to miss classes and school days, continue to be disruptive, continue to get suspended, and continue to screw up. Sometimes they squeak by, sometimes they drop out, and sometimes, sadly, they even wind up incarcerated. The numbers can be bent a billion different ways but in the end there seems little doubt, at least in the United States, that many of those who wind up behind bars arrive there after a lifetime of poor performance, or poor socialization in school.

Yet even the most cursory discussion with just about any student will reveal that students can, as can most of us, explain which choices are "better" and which are "worse." However, knowing better choices and being capable and committed to making better choices are really two different skills. This is where the importance of engagement plays a part.

Any neophyte teacher can see at a glance that a great many students can see what needs to be done in the short term to accomplish what they want in the long term, but fewer are able to act on it in a positive way. What is so simple and so stark, so clear and so compelling is that students who can understand this relationship, and are willing to do what they must do, develop the habit of being successful students and become successful students.

The writer Peter DeVries, while noting that he was not particularly impressed by them, observed that all Ivy League schools really did was "take the best students in the country and turn them into the best students in the country." To a large extent, in our schools, it's mostly what we do also: make successful students into successful students, and then send some of them (all the ones who were in my class anyway) off to Yale, Harvard, Columbia, Cornell, and Princeton and the rest to . . . well . . . wherever.

This takes away nothing from the genuine excellence, or even the brilliance, of many of these students. Many of the kids who fill the seats in the more challenging classes are unusually bright, and unusually capable, but just as many, if not more, test out in the generally average range but have developed the ability to be good at school.

This is not a negative. In fact, what they are doing is exactly right: they are applying *critical success skills* to accomplish something that is important to them. However, at the same time there are tons and tons and tons of exceptionally bright kids out there who have developed excellence at screwing up and continue to do so in spite of all the times they have been "told" that they are headed for disaster. Facilitative teachers, having helped students define a clear vision or goal, now must engage students in the difficult action of using such desire to change habits.

At a principal interview in a high-performing high school in a wealthy community, a parent asked a potential candidate if he truly felt equipped, having come from an urban (read: predominately minority population), lower-performing high school, to be able to be a principal in a school with parents who "cared more about their children" and were more committed to their children's success.

Setting aside, for the moment, the offensive nature of such a comment, what such a comment reveals is how little this woman understood the difference between having a dream—and even having a commitment to that dream—and having the wherewithal, both personal and financial, to bring that dream to fruition. And that is exactly a key part of *The Missing Link*.

Successful people often have successful children . . . but why?

In part it is because successful parents can simply create the pathways for their children (to paraphrase the Led Zeppelin song, they can buy the stairway to heaven). There is no dearth of tales of the offspring of the wealthy who are rescued from their interminable screw-ups by the family's wealth and power until they are finally placed in jobs they can't screw up: like being the figurehead officer of a major league baseball team in charge of taking politicians to lunch.

But that's an extreme example. For the most part successful people have successful children because they *engage* their children in learning, either through direct instruction or indirectly by example, the successful habits that lead to success. Among these habits, which again will be examined with greater focus moving forward, are such traits as: decision-making, organization, persistence, appropriate social skills, and, most importantly, self-regulation.

It doesn't take a big brain to see that observable actions in adults, especially parents, sometimes find their way into the actions of the children they influence. A couple who had regularly engaged in exercise but had never required their children to participate found that as their sons became adults, they made healthful exercise a part of their regular routines as well.

Behaviors can be learned from those significant others who engage in those behaviors. This simple "engagement" osmosis figures prominently into the lives of successful adults: for the rest, such learning must come either from other influential adults (among whom, of consummate importance, are professional educators) or through the sometimes-painful trial and error born of sheer desperation. But while engagement in learning habit may just happen at home, at school it does not just happen. It must be made to happen.

3. COMMUNICATE!

Nowhere is the need to communicate meaningfully more critical than in the classroom and in school. Parental relationships, while still requiring meaningful communication, are simply less time driven and so can evolve over a longer period. Teachers who intend to help students develop habits that change their lives, rather than merely move them along toward the same outcomes, have to rethink the teacher-talk-centered approach employed as the main teaching and guidance strategy. Teaching success skills requires a greater degree of careful, active listening, and interactive communication, rather than merely talking at kids, which is what mostly happens.

Many instructional supervisors have become more and more aware of just how much teacher talk there is versus the amount of meaningful student talk during instructional time. Setting aside the occasionally *well-executed* cooperative learning activity, the amount of learning-related student talk time is generally scarce (unfortunately many poorly planned cooperative learning activities devolve into nonpurposeful student chatting, especially if the teacher uses the time to catch up on paperwork at his or her desk).

A recent study of three math teachers found that over several months they talked an average of almost 75 percent of class time, which seems to agree with the common wisdom of the percentage of teacher talk versus student talk. Even in so-called discussions, teachers are often gatekeepers to all student interactions.

In most classrooms, student talk is engendered by teacher inquiry. Typically, at some point the teacher will pose a question to assess student learning, or sometimes to engage students in the inquiry process itself. Even assuming the latter, that in fact the teacher's intent is to foster student discussion, in most cases the ratio of teacher talk to student talk is not significantly different. The teacher asks a question; a student selected by the teacher responds. Assuming it is a complex, higher-order thinking question, in a best-case scenario, it most often engenders a response typically briefer than the amount of time used for formulating the question being asked.

In response, the teacher then constructs a response to the student's response, usually in the form of a critique as to why the answer was correct or incorrect. Generally the teacher will then follow up by formulating yet another question. Sometimes following up, sometimes on a new topic entirely to continue to engender student responses to which, again, a single student called on by the teacher responds and on, and on, and on.

Thus over about a ten-minute period, in a best-case scenario, it's not hard to get above the 70 percent teacher-talk level. Extrapolate this over a whole day, over a whole week, or over a whole year and it is no wonder that very little change occurs in the lives of students who tend to be unaffected by their learning experiences. Even the ancient Chinese understood this as defined by this proverb: "Tell me and I forget; show me and I may remember; involve me and I will understand."

In getting students to adopt this more deeply proactive and self-directed approach to achievement, personal engagement in the process is critical. Facilitating students, rather than directing them, invites students into a process where they can identify what they really want, and then engage in applying success skills to achieve these outcomes. Quite simply, this involves a different, more communicative approach to relating to students. However, getting to this different dynamic involves mere adjustments rather than radical change.

A teacher's role is to help all students learn, not just those few who key into their particular teaching styles or personal concepts of what qualifies a student (and a student's dream) of being "worthy." Most teachers do this willingly and regularly, but not necessarily effectively, especially with students who come to school not fully capable of being successful. To be effective in teaching critical success skills in particular, teachers and administrators will need to rethink long-established roles.

Teachers who wish to help students truly find *their own* way must get the hell out of the *judgment* business and get into the *facilitation* business, pure and simple. The function of a modern teacher in our very changed society demands this "coaching" approach to engender student engagement and success. Kids *are* different today, and trying to teach them with the system that worked for students of the past simply no longer works as well.

Our job as professionals is very clear: stop discussing how kids have changed and start changing to meet the needs of our kids. The essence of being professionals implies the ability to change, to embrace new technologies and new relationships, while still maintaining the core values through which we can maintain orderly schools and engage in highly effective teaching. The new dynamics merely moves schooling from a structure dominated by educator intentions for students to a structure driven by student intentions for themselves. High-performing schools and classrooms, particularly those schools that have served "professional" communities, have always done this.

The means of facilitative interaction with students, explored in subsequent chapters, is not complex, though it does take some practice. However, in such a facilitative structure these critical success skills can also be employed as a teaching/school-management tool. As students embrace and internalize these practices, it can work to dynamically change the way students feel about themselves and their potential. When students take more positive command of their own lives, and make better long- and short-term decisions, it makes the lives of educators that much better as well.

THREE

Either We Act as a Family, or Forget It

There is that term almost every teacher, if not every student, has heard from the very beginning of their educational careers. *In loco parentis.* Roughly translated it simply means the person in place of a parent, *the near parent*. Rooted in ancient cultures, when children were indeed raised, more or less, by a closely knit, like-thinking village of similarly valued parents, it denotes the responsibility of each adult to act as the parent, if the actual parent is not present, of whichever child is near and in need of parenting. In our modern construct it is the tenet of law that empowers those in charge of children, primarily teachers, school administrators, and even police, to act *with the authority* of a parent in place of the parent. Essentially parents agree to allow significant parental authority to be designated to others while their child is involved in school and related activities.

This relationship is so powerful in fact that few courts are willing to challenge the structure. In one case the Supreme Court even stated that they were purposely providing wide berth to schools in decision-making regarding the well-being of students. The justices made it clear that were they to even crack the door to adjudicating disputes between parents and schools, and students and schools, the court would have little time for anything else.

This makes perfect sense, of course. School administrators understand that to maintain order in the school, they must have fairly broad authority to act even outside the strict domain of the school building. In one instance, middle school administrators had to become involved in a social media entanglement that was threatening to erupt in the school itself.

When these social media interactions among a group of boys and girls began to cross the line into bullying and confrontation in and near the school, the principal invoked his authority to intervene and suspended all the students involved until their parents could be brought together for a meeting with school officials and the students.

Parents of many of the students, as well as the students themselves, claimed administrators had no such authority to discipline these students for their actions outside of school, and though several threatened legal action, their attorneys quickly disabused them of those notions. The need for parental authority for teachers, administrators, and school personnel in classrooms and in the school environs is critical to assure the safe and orderly conduct of school. Without this authority school cannot function properly, let alone to hope for any actual learning to take place.

While teaching *critical success skills* aims at empowering students to take control of their lives and futures, for unequivocal clarity's sake, please recognize that neither schools nor teachers will be or should be giving up their authority. *It is critical that parents and significant others have and maintain clear authority over the lives of their children.* However, engaging children to have some limited autonomy over themselves, while maintaining authority, is a stellar idea that has been grossly misapplied and poorly practiced as permissiveness.

No less an authority on child development than Dr. Benjamin Spock bewailed this misinterpretation of his limited child autonomy prescription. Responding to the notion that the freewheeling attitudes of the 1960s and 1970s were a direct result of his teachings, he unequivocally stated that he had never advocated "permissive anything" and that persons stating otherwise completely misunderstood his ideas. He stated that he advocated only treating a child as a person, with his or her own feelings, hopes, dreams. "The child supplies the power," said Dr. Spock, "but the parents have to do the steering."

Parents and educators who engage their children in limited forms of decision-making are in fact teaching decision-making. On the other hand, parents who abdicate their authority, for whatever reason, effectually rob children of their necessary structure, the context in which all good decisions are made. Parents who are good teachers (professional teachers are supposed to know this) intuitively understand that good teaching is about understanding and application. Lecture alone may create knowledge, but it is practice that creates the applicatory skills.

In schools, developing an opportunity for students to internalize and apply critical success skills involves a measure of freedom, within a clear, consistent structure. To do this, *in loco parentis* as an expression of authority alone misses the mark. Authority alone, structure alone, consequences alone, simply do not teach. If it did, suspensions and incarcerations would be one to a customer, which, in fact, is not the current recidivism rate.

A perfect example of this lecture limitation occurred during a youth soccer game. The coach, another parent, had been recruited for the job because he had been a soccer player in college and so was deemed uniquely equipped to lead these six-year-olds to victory. With a seriousness of purpose suitable to a World Cup match, the coach created two rectangles on his marker board and began to explain to a scum of children the value of an offensive attack that employed this geometric strategy of ball control.

They listened, and when they were asked if they understood they all nodded. They politely stood where the coach placed them, but once the whistle blew, the lecture went right out the window and, like most children's sporting contests, it was strictly *Lord of the Flies*. Packs of wild children in expensive uniforms, in clusters bearing little relationship to geometric logic, chased the ball all over the field hacking away at each other with flailing arms and legs.

Parents who are good teachers, and good teachers, provide their children with the always-increasing foundation of decision-making and personal behavior knowledge on which they build and build. They do this by offering examples of the behaviors they expect, as well as by having expectations of their own children's behaviors. More critically they capitalize on opportunities to learn and practice successful behaviors at appropriate times and in appropriate ways.

A high school freshman auditioned for a regional "all-star" orchestra and then, when accepted, balked at the idea of joining, claiming that his already-packed schedule left little enough time for fun already. His parents decided to allow him to make his own decision about joining but created a context to make that decision. They asked him if he still enjoyed playing, which he said he did. They also asked him if he was still interested in going to the conservatory college he had been expressing the desire to attend, to which he responded he was. Finally, though they intended to ask him to connect how being a member of such an orchestra would impact on increasing his skills, before they got to it the child had determined that the sacrifice made sense now and, of course, went on to join the orchestra.

Families that function well offer these experiential opportunities within consistent boundaries, with common language, and with clear and meaningful consequences that are enforced in compassionate ways. On the other hand, families without consistency do not often teach self-discipline, or structure or boundaries or much else that will help their child find useful independence.

Instead they learn finding the path of least resistance, expedience, no boundaries, and worst of all, no real consequences. What their children learn is how to manipulate, how to split, how to get what they want in the easiest way possible. Fortunately for them the lack of meaningful communication among professionals in schools creates ample opportunity for getting by, and frequently, kids who can manipulate manage quite well in school. At least well enough to graduate but perhaps not well enough to actually learn success skills.

Families that don't function really well have a great deal in common with the structure of schools, as exemplified in figure 3.1, below. Clearly, though the child is in the "main focus," unfortunately, because the child is the only one receiving all the communication, the child is also, essentially, in charge. Most political leaders recognize the power inherent in controlling communication. So do kids.

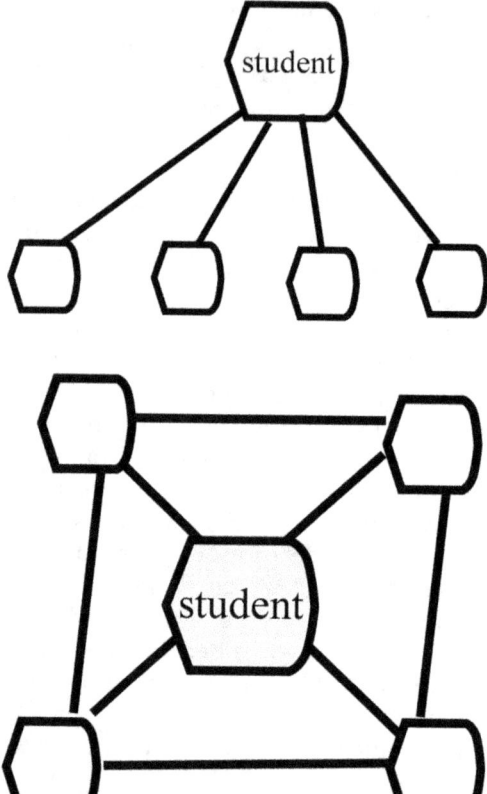

Figure 3.1.

Figure 3.2.

In families than function well (figure 3.2), *public* agreement (i.e., the child gets a single, consistent message that is worked out by the adult in private) among those responsible informs "important" interactions with the children. Also, clearly, the adults not only communicate with the child but also communicate with each other.

In respect of less functional families, as to the question of who's in charge of the children, the simple answer is that it could be anybody, even if it is the same person. Dad does "this" one day and something else another; dad says one thing, but mom says another. Homework before play, homework after play, homework why bother. What's right or wrong, what's effective or ineffective, what's yes or no is as changeable as the wind.

Kind of sounds like school—doesn't it?

On a train to New York City a superintendent of a local school district observed two mothers, each with a child about the same age and gender. The circus was in town, and both of these families were off to enjoy it after a train ride of about forty-five minutes. The interactions between the two mothers and their two children really typify this consistency.

One of the mothers, as the child's boredom started to make her fidget and begin to act out, started out by mollifying ("We'll be there soon") and quickly moved to correction: "Sit still." "Stop whining." "Stay in your seat." "I'll make a deal with you. If you can sit still all the way to New York you can have popcorn and candy." Soon after came consequences. "If you don't start behaving, we're going to go right home!" "One more time I have to speak to you, and you can forget any treats at the circus."

The other mother engaged with her daughter in discussing the circus, and to the child's increasing excitement, diverted her attention to books she had brought, identifying scenery and discussing all the way-cool things she would be seeing and experiencing at the circus. "Do you think those elephants are going to be big or small?"

Anybody want to bet which of these two children is likely to be successful in school? This is not to say that parents must be perfect, but neither should a parent be twenty different people.

Differently than families, in many instances consistency among teachers and from classroom to classroom may not be necessary but when it is, the likelihood of getting it is highly unlikely. A not-too-infrequent remark heard from more than one teacher was that they didn't have to do anything they didn't want to do. "What're they going to do, write me up? They can't fire me: I've got tenure!"

But this intransigent attitude is not the fault of teachers alone. Frequently messages to teachers are vague and contradictory, sometimes even coming from the same administrator who decrees one policy one day and the exact opposite the next day, if not actually in the same sentence. Often policy is dictated and altered at so many levels, from supervisors right up the chain to superintendents and boards of education and mayors and presidents, that it ends up on the desks of teachers as little more than an anxiety-provoking muddle. The oft-described "initiative fatigue" (the mental and emotional exhaustion of having truly invested in some sort of program with the belief that it will be long term and meaningful only to have it abandoned for the next initiative) is particularly problematic for well-meaning teachers who actually invest deeply in trying to follow these pinball-shifting initiatives.

Frequently poorly planned policy is the result of *headliners*, leaders who read the headlines and book flaps but never bother to acquaint themselves with the nuances of an initiative. One principal, for instance, created a professional learning community (PLC), which is normally designed to produce deep investigation of specific instructional practices by a small group of teachers meeting frequently. In this school the PLC consisted of more than thirty teachers assigned to meet for half an hour, once a week, which proved fruitless and ineffective.

Like the boy who cried wolf, poorly planned or insufficiently rooted policy and strategy do little to promote any future deep investment in change that might produce meaningful improvement in student outcomes. Few families that offer the level of contradictory direction that is offered in schools produce children sufficiently focused on successful practices to make much headway, at least in the academic world. Somewhere along the way, a child who becomes successful gets a successful message. It may not come from parents, but it comes from somewhere.

This clarity of policy, and a genuine long-range investment in change, must be a part of any plan that seeks to establish and hone the reception and internalization of student success skills. *As stated at the outset, this is not a quick fix.* The complexity of learning these skills, as opposed to, say, the simpler learning of a *thing* (like how to identify a "distracter" on a standardized test), simply takes more time, more patience, more commitment, and ultimately, more compassion. Unfortunately, this is the wall into which we frequently run.

WHAT DOES SUCCESSFUL PARENTING ENTAIL, AND WHY SHOULD THIS BE THE SCHOOL'S RESPONSIBILITY?

It is the parents' job to give their children a strong success foundation, absolutely. No disagreement here. But in the absence of parenting that helps students succeed, professional educators must make a choice: they can either throw up their hands or throw down the gauntlet. Meaning they can either become the "parent" that helps a student succeed or just pass that kid on to the next grade, the next teacher, or the next event.

The concept of in loco parentis asks teachers to act as the parent in the absence of the parent. But to help students develop positive, life-long habits, in loco parentis cannot just be about the use of authority alone. If professional educators are going to act in such a way as to build capacity, instead of just employing the capacity that is already there, teachers must act as the near parent *with parental compassion* as well as parental authority.

Successful parents raise their children with what can be called *courageous compassion*, not just with the enforcement of blind authority. Rather, what good parents do is use their authority judiciously, as an expression of the values they want to teach.

Abraham Lincoln understood this, famously stating that "nearly all men can stand adversity, but if you want to test a man's character, give him power." Thus, the parent who takes off his or her belt to teach their child not to bully his or her younger sibling is surely delivering a lesson, but the true objective is doubtless a very different learning objective than the one that parent thinks he or she is teaching.

Courageous compassion is that ability to apply thoughtful authority as a part of a teaching process whereby instruction, choice, and consequence are married to produce meaningful opportunities to learn. It is also the willingness to employ this instructional process even when the timing may create great stress. There are zillions of examples that happen every day in homes all over the world, examples great and small.

Ever stand at the door with the clock ticking while little Johnny dawdles with his untied shoelaces? When children are given an opportunity to make a choice, and parents have taken the time to talk through the options in respect of possible outcomes, courageously compassionate parents have the guts to both let the child choose and assure that the consequences of the choice are not mollified. Too much parental rescuing, as we have outlined earlier, actually robs children of their self-efficacy. In other words, if you plan on tying little Johnny's shoes every time you get frustrated, you might as well just buy him shoes with Velcro straps now and get it over with.

One parent, having had several conversations regarding underaged drinking, allowed her child to stay in jail (albeit at a local precinct house in a suburban community) because they had warned of just such a consequence. What made this a courageous choice, apart from the fact that all of the other parents bailed out their children immediately, was the fact that having to enforce this consequence made this parent so anxious she was virtually ill. Eight sleepless hours later, when she came to get him released from the precinct, her son was (as expected) pretty angry, but he also eventually understood the clear message of real consequences for real choices. He understood that in the real world there just might be some situations that his parents might not be able to fix.

However, holding kids accountable is just one element of courageous compassion, at least as we apply it as parents and professionals. It is the willingness not to fix everything, but it is also having the guts to let a process evolve, albeit with instruction and guidance. And this can be tough, especially when it affects your kids, or when your time is so drawn that any boondoggle can be overwhelming. A perfect example happened to a high school administrator in charge of a senior class.

A student, a young lady, showed up in his office in tears certain that she had failed one of her classes because she had been unable to complete an exam in the allotted time. The administrator knew this student to be a pretty good student who, though she hadn't been in any serious trouble, was a little quick to become frustrated and angry. He also assessed that the teacher involved happened to be a fairly malleable fellow who most often would put the needs of his students first. The administrator realized in an instant that he could fix the problem with a single phone call right then and there.

Given the level of his stress, arranging all the details of assuring academic completion of graduation requirements, as well as the graduation ceremony of close to four hundred students, his first instinct was to just make the call and be done with it. But his classroom instinct, recognizing a teachable moment, kicked in. So while he knew that the most expedient course would be to just fix it, his *teacherly* side forced him to act with courageous compassion.

"Well," he asked, "what do you want to do about it?"

"I want to go right up there and tell him to let me finish the exam! He has no right to keep me from graduating," she said, her voice rising. "*He didn't give us enough time!*"

"Ok, so let's follow this plan through. You go to the teacher and demand he let you complete the test. How do you think he'll respond?"

"I don't know. I need to finish that test!"

"Well, how do you respond when someone gets up in your face?"

"Yeah, right . . . not so well."

"So, do you think he'll respond any differently?"

Eventually, the administrator was able to calm her and focus on developing a plan. Though her fall-back position always seemed to be confrontation, the administrator kept her focused on empathy and questions that forced her to think ahead. Most importantly, when she ventured into her anger the administrator kept asking her to take such an action to its possible conclusions, which she invariably recognized as having a poor outcome.

"How do you want this interaction to turn out? What do you want? Do you think that kind of decision will get you to the outcome you want?"

Eventually she determined, with some surreptitious guidance, that since in the end what she really wanted was the opportunity to complete the exam, and to get done with high school, a more conciliatory rather than a more confrontational approach might produce the best results. They practiced this approach, as well, with the administrator playing the role of the teacher, and after several false starts, she was able to create a cogent, convincing argument that was, at one in the same time, both compelling and nonthreatening.

In the end, just as he expected, the teacher had no problem giving the student a little extra time, and would probably have done so right at the time had she not stormed angrily out of the room. Having completed and passed the exam, the student met all of her requirements and graduated. Best of all, everybody won!

The student, as she told the administrator, felt great being able to connect with the teacher on a human level, and the teacher was willing and happy to help her solve the problem. And, as the administrator said, if that moment didn't do enough for his own professional pride, when he greeted this student on the graduation dais, she shook his hand, kissed him on the cheek, and said, "Thank you so much. You taught me something I'll remember for the rest of my life!"

Here then was the result of a single, individualized, success-skill-driven lesson where the student was able to learn and apply and perhaps, even in a rudimentary way, begin to internalize a practice that might lead to future interpersonal successes. Certainly anyone who has even dipped a toe into the employment market in the last thirty years recognizes the critical importance of having honed appropriate workplace social skills. Most importantly, the student got to be the hero of her own story. Nothing was fixed for her: she succeeded and because she now had a moment of success, she became a little more empowered. And the entire investment on the part of the administrator was less than the length of a basic lesson: perhaps twenty minutes.

Lastly, and even more importantly, *courageous compassion* is also about having the courage to move the line when necessary. The frequently misconstrued Emerson quote is not that consistency, but rather a *false* consistency, "is the hobgoblin of small minds." Teachers, administrators, and parents need to be able to measure when veering from the program is in the best interests of the child, and when it is not. It is often difficult to know, but perhaps, as we move along, we will be able to shed some light on the nuances of such decisions. For now, or so it seems, in both parenting and education, zero-tolerance rules produce nothing but zero thinking and, historically, zero thinking has never been the cause of anyone becoming more learned.

FAMILIAL STRUCTURES THAT WORK IN SCHOOLS: A CASE FOR THE "CLINICAL" MODEL

Imagine, then, that the previously referenced interaction was not a rare one, or one that occurred at a last-moment transition from one world to another. Imagine instead that this is the ethos and actions of everyone: that from day one of school students are taught, trained, and then, finally, expected to behave in ways that exemplify the best employment of these success skills.

The unfortunate reality is that in most schools there is an *expectation* of these behaviors but sore little in the way of actually teaching them. They are spoken of, and lectured about, but professionals should not mistake "delivering" instruction as an indication that learning has taken place as well.

As with any other learning, before expecting such behaviors we ought first to teach them, and while everyone is 100 percent in favor of making parents perfect, what exactly are we supposed to do if parents deliver us students that are not as well developed as we would like? One educational staff developer sarcastically remarked to a group of teachers, complaining that the instructional methods she was suggesting simply could not be done with their particular kids: "Well, I do understand how these difficult kids are keeping you from being able to teach successfully, but unfortunately, these were the only kids these parents had to send to school. They aren't keeping all the better ones at home!"

The radical departure here recognizes the need to develop at the school level an operational structure that, while not duplicating the consistent and compassionately authoritative nature of the highly functional family structure, tries to approximate and replicate what is important in that structure for learning and internalizing the practice of these success skills.

What that means is that we must focus on teaching these critical success skills, and in the creating of a familial-like consistency, but not on usurping parental authority. Fortunately, teaching critical skills does not necessarily need to be as values based as are many so called character-education programs.

But still, in our role as teachers (at least as John Dewey defined it), and the role of the school, is to be instrumental in the creation of individuals and in forming our children to be members of our larger society. As Dewey wrote, "Education is not preparation for life, it is life itself!" Because of that, teachers and schools have much and have always had much latitude to apply the thoughtful teaching of accepted communal values. James Baldwin's understanding of how to educate in a meaningful way is applicable here, though he was specifically referring to how African American students could use their education to subvert society's institutionally racist intent. "We must," he said, "learn the tools and then educate ourselves."

The powerful structural, technological, and economic changes in our society that have created the need to develop self-reliant citizens have also made it mandatory for schools to teach these critical success skills as a "professional family."

As represented earlier in figure 3.1, a typical school structure seems to replicate the character of a less consistent family. In this model, the student tends to interact as an independent agent with a series of independent agents. She or he relies on the fact that professional communication between and among the interconnected parties is sparse and, for the most part, not very substantive.

Unfortunately, most schools are still stuck in the long-outdated industrial model where internal workings of each stage are, for the most part, independent of the internal working of the next stage. So long as the appropriate part is where it needs to be when it moves down the line, how it got there is almost entirely irrelevant. So when Khadria passes English 9 with a 78 percent, social studies with an 83 percent, and math by the skin of her teeth, she is just moved right down the conveyor belt for another round of the same in tenth grade. In most schools these final grades, and maybe attendance, are just about all her next teacher is going to know about Khadria.

This industrial model on which our persistently difficult-to-change school structure was formed was one that fostered the creation of goods dictated for a market driven by a freedom from consumer protections that was afforded industrial barons. This made moot the condition under which a part was made, or even the quality of that part. So long as, once it was attached the car, it ran well enough to be sold, once it was sold, *caveat emptor*: let the buyer beware!

Modern industrial constructs, recognizing the need for better controls to increase efficiency and quality, have moved away from such rigid industrial arrangements into a world of information sharing and interdependence. Many schools are also beginning to understand the critical importance of working as a team, just as is done in virtually every hospital and clinic everywhere. A simple fantasy of imaging a hospital run like most schools more than tells the tale.

A patient goes to the emergency room, his dog having nipped his fingertip. A nurse in triage takes his information, meticulously, including his mortal allergy to antibiotics. After he is moved along to the treating physician, his information is carefully filed and, essentially, unavailable. The doctor recognizes that this is a case of nipped finger and, in addition to a numbing shot and stitches, he also administers an antibiotic to prevent infection, which, unfortunately, puts the patient into immediate cardiac arrest. Need I go on?

This lack of information-sharing, which would be criminally negligent in any hospital, is pretty much the standard of care in most schools. Well-functioning families, many of whom employ and build success skills in their children, share information regularly. So should functional schools. By doing so, schools will be able to put the kid squarely in the center and in charge of his or her own education, but not in charge of the school. Given the great amount of technology available, much of this interconnection can be done, efficiently and securely, right online, right now, with little or no expense.

However, the current reality is that student records are still primarily paper based and generally limited to recording, other than attendance and grades, administrative actions only. They are also usually only available to administrators, and their support staff, as well. Yet the most cursory assessment of any school will reveal that, on a daily basis, the vast majority of adult-student interactions take place with teachers, not administrators. How, then, are we to approach structures to teach self-discipline and self-regulation and decision-making as a *professional family*?

To communicate meaningfully with each other about our students, and to successfully recreate the relational family structure in schools, sharing information cannot feel like another "thing" teachers and administrators will have to do. Just as in a clinical setting, the relationship between sharing information and seeing success has to be clear and meaningful. The key is to identify what is important to know, regarding teacher-student interactions, and what is less important so that records can be done quickly but meaningfully.

This kind of information is particularly important if, say, a teacher, using thoughtful, professional judgment, decides not to enforce a consequence because he or she sees it as being in the best interest of a student. Knowing that Ms. Williams decided not to enforce detention for Sally's being significantly late to a class because she whispered to Ms. Williams the cause of the lateness was to prevent an accident of a personal nature might just be the kind of measured response that is entirely acceptable. However, it is also important to know when such a "break" has been given for Sally on the off chance that she may be late for another class tomorrow and yet another class another time. Each adult in thoughtful kindnesses would most probably excuse the rarely late Sally. However, if this kind of information is shared, we allow ourselves the ability to be understanding while reducing the chances of our being manipulated by a master tactician taking advantage of the fact that none of us communicates.

There is a real struggle among professionals to balance all the elements of one's professional and personal life, but communicating with each other, and agreeing to be committed to one set of community values, must be a priority. Prioritizing this kind of agreement and communication reflects the value we place in these skills, and becomes true expression of the value of having our students learn these skills. Later we will also see how using the power of technology can make this information collection simple, efficient, and easily shared.

ROUNDS: HOW IS THIS GOING TO WORK?

In an emergency room in a hospital a man is brought in, clearly in distress, but unable to communicate much about his condition. He is taken immediately into an examination area, where there is a flurry of medical activity. After about twenty minutes, during which time an enormous amount of data is collected by several individuals, suddenly the whole attending team gets called into a huddle. After that brief conference, the frenzy ended and a methodical diagnostic plan began to evolve that in short order led to a focused treatment plan.

To be sure the frenetic activity was important: they had to be sure his condition was not immediately life threatening, but had they stayed on that same path the disparate information they collected might not have been collated and a thorough diagnosis made. What is remarkable is how little we apply this unified, focused approach to the plans we make concerning the lives and learning of children in school. Indeed the frenetic activity and lack of communication that defined the initial stages of this man's visit to the emergency room often continue all throughout a child's years in school. The first move is to change that.

There are lots of very simple ways to accomplish this, and any suggestions contained herein are just suggestions and not intended to be offered as the only structure that might work. One such structure is called the *Power of Ten*.

Briefly, the Power of Ten is a concept developed in several urban schools where one professional in the building took on the "mentorship" of ten individual students. Ten, it turns out, is often the average ratio of students to adults in most schools. The intention was to augment guidance services that, in this school as in most schools, were pretty overwhelmed. In some schools guidance counselors carry a caseload of several hundred students each year.

The simple bottom line was that all each adult had to do was check in once a week or so (less, if warranted, more if necessary) with his or her mentee after first checking the mentee's weekly record. To be clear a certain amount of training and practice was conducted, assuring that these folks were knowledgeable about how to mentor effectively.

This arrangement was able to serve two key functions. Most importantly it provided a single individual for each student who was interested and invested in his or her success. Secondarily, it also provided the professional staff with a single individual who could provide a critical and clinical overview that would, like the huddle in the emergency room, offer a clearer means for better planning for our students' learning and their lives.

So, how does this help me teach these success skills?

Glad you asked.

Because these success skills are a series of habits to be developed rather than ideas to be learned, the ability to have a community of consistent feedback is of absolutely monumental importance. While it is true that these skills are mentioned frequently and demanded constantly, little is done to actually tie together expectation, knowledge, and ability. Lots of people *know how* to play basketball as well as Michael Jordan, but only Michael Jordan can actually play as well as Michael Jordan.

You get the picture: you can talk about arithmetic until you're blue in the face but until you get a kid to take cotton balls in and out of a single bowl in the math center, the concept of addition and subtraction may be pretty hard to comprehend. Guided and independent practice has assumed a rightful place in the pantheon of best practices because it works. However, it should be very clear that the more complex the learning expectations, the more complex the instruction will have to be, and the more protracted the learning process will be as well.

This clinical approach does for the entire learning community what guided and independent instruction does for a specific classroom: it allows learners to embrace, practice, and internalize a complex set of behaviors. When the school becomes a single milieu, as in a clinical setting, then from classroom to classroom, on the sports field and in the theater, at school and at home the message is clear, unified, and consistent:

- Life is about choices.
- Successful lives are about successful choices.
- Stop, think ahead, ask the critical question of how will this (action I am about to undertake) affect my ability to reach my stated goals, and only then, act.
- How can I keep moving in the right direction even after I've made an error?

This will seem cumbersome at first simply because creating new habits, for staff as well as students, is a time-dense activity. Savvy administrators working with the input of their faculty can also devise clear expectations for what teachers are expected to know and do and say (using, for instance, qualitatively oriented rubrics) as well as systems for staff to have constant and consistent input in refining the system.

Quickly, though, such behaviors do become habit, attended to in nanoseconds, but this time we are investing in creating the habit of success rather than the habit of failure. That's the nature of learning, folks, and it is the coin of our educational realm: what we seek to sell we ought to both exemplify as well as model.

When all the adults and (especially) all of the students who interact with each other on a regular basis all key in on the same message, with the same language, in a way that supports autonomous but highly successful personal choices, we will have become what we have intended to become: a supportive, functional family. This is the ultimate goal. And if you don't believe that a familial community committed to each member making positive short-term choices in respect of grand desires they have for the future can have a meaningful positive impact on achievement, merely ask Drs. Davis, Jenkins, and Hunt, authors of *The Pact*, to weigh in on this idea or merely read their compelling story. You will find that they agree.

FOUR
Buying In Is the Easy Part

> You have to expect things of yourself before you can do them.
> —Michael Jordan
>
> Long before I became a success, my parents made me feel like I could be one. —Toni Morrison

Ask students on the first day of school what grade they would like for the year. Ask them to fill out an index card with a bunch of information you might not even need (parental contact numbers, email addresses, etc.) just to get them to not be wary, so they might write down a grade with as little thinking as you can get. Almost invariably some student will ask for a definition. "Do you mean the grade we think we're going to get, or the one we want?"

Implore them not to think about past experience, or what habit has caused them to think is likely will occur, but rather to merely dream, unencumbered by reality. Ask if they could just wake up next June and have that grade, what would that grade be? You can guess that except for a wag who will say s/he actually wants an *F* (usually rescinded when asked if that's really true) all of the students claim to want a *B* or an *A*. This is the joy of new beginnings, the unreality of hope over experience (ask anyone about that who has been married for the second or third time).

Although you can never go back and make a new beginning, to paraphrase Carl Bard, you can always start from anywhere and make a new end. This turnaround becomes powerful when we can help our students, and ourselves, apply the lessons of our past in a thoughtful way that actually produces positive change moving forward. It is simple to understand of course, but hard as hell to apply.

The reality is on the first day of school everyone wants to pass, to succeed, but some will, unfortunately, not see themselves through on the promise they have made to themselves.

Similarly, it is not difficult to get students of any age to recognize the importance of developing successful habits: in fact, it is a relatively simple undertaking that can be taught in the time it takes to understand a poem such as "Autobiography in Five Short Chapters" by Portia Nelson. The poem is widely available and one students seem to enjoy, and one they seem to be able to easily access and understand. However, if understanding what to do was enough, the prisons would be all empty and, happily, out of business.

Nelson's brief poem employs a metaphor of self-discovery expressed through a series of walks down the same street. Initially the narrator falls into a hole and must struggle to extricate herself while denying responsibility for having fallen in to begin with. Yet she keeps walking down the same street and falling into the same hole. It is, she notes, a habit. Subsequently she recognizes her own responsibility for her fate, extricates herself more quickly each time, and eventually learns first to avoid the hole and then, finally, to find a different street.

Students seem to notice and articulate several things quickly. Chiefly they see and relate to the narrator in this poem. The speaker lives a life not too different from most kids (most of us, one day or another)—walking down the same street, falling into the same hole over and over and over. The difficult part, however, is what is not in the poem, what gets in the way of applying this simple idea: how we can avoid the same pitfalls over and over again.

"Habit," says Vladimir, a character in Samuel Beckett's *Waiting for Godot*, "is a great deadener." Habit takes the place of thinking way more than we probably want. To some extent, that is life. If we had to think through every single decision to its conclusion, life would be a very slow chess game: ponderous hours of decision-making interspersed with nanoseconds of action. Habit certainly makes quick work of certain elements of our life, like getting ready for work, and allows us to save such thinking time for more weighty issues, such as what to eat for lunch.

However, habit can also freeze our senses and foster an inability to engage with our own lives. "I sometimes feel like I am on one of those walkway thingies at the airport," remarked one student, "just going where it takes me whether I like it or not."

We move along rather than make forward-going choices about how we want to live, becoming, in effect, the exact opposite of Cassius, in Shakespeare's *Julius Caesar*, who implores Brutus that the fault lies "not within the stars, but within ourselves, that we are underlings."

To play further with Shakespeare's words, "men at some time are masters of their fate," but not always. And of course we all make mistakes. But as we will further understand, especially when working with learners, recognizing without criminalizing mistakes is part of developing success skills. The narrator's realization that he or she bears some responsibility for winding up in the hole again empowers the speaker to get out of the hole more quickly, but most importantly it is also the beginning of a very powerful lesson for the reader that is open to seeing it.

LEARNED HELPLESSNESS: A BRIEF OVERVIEW

A man wears a mask, and his face grows to fit it. —George Orwell

In early 1965, Martin Seligman and his colleagues, while studying the relationship between fear and learning, accidentally discovered an unexpected phenomenon while doing experiments on dogs using Pavlovian (classical) conditioning.

As surely you have seen in yourself, like dogs, when presented with food (sometimes even thinking about food!), we salivate. Pavlov discovered that if he repeatedly rang a bell with this presentation of food, he could condition the dog to pair the sound with the food. Eventually, the bell itself produced exactly the same level of salivation in the dog as it did when the food was presented. Seligman's theory was that fear could be conditioned just as could hunger.

He built a dog house with two rooms separated by a small wall, a wall that the dog could easily jump over if he so chose. He then took a lovable, furry little doggy and gave it a shock (Seligman claimed it was harmless but there are reports that one of the dogs begged, "Don't taze me, Bro!"). The normal dog response to such a shock was, not surprisingly, to leap over the wall into the "safety" of the next room. In virtually every single instance these dogs did exactly what most would do in the face of such impending discomfort or pain: we'd get the hell out!

After having established normal dog response, Seligman then began the learning phase. Seligman and his colleagues restrained the dogs in the front room in a kind of a hammock, or sling, which allowed for little movement. Thus tied up, he gave the dogs their shocks accompanied by the ringing bell. The expectation was that after the dog learned to associate the electric shock with the bell, just as with Pavlov's experiment, fear could be engendered with the ringing of the bell alone. Upon hearing it, they hypothesized, the dog would leap to safety as he had at the outset. Only that's not what happened.

Instead of leaping to safety the conditioned dog just pathetically laid down, whimpering and expecting his portion of pain and misery. Seligman had conditioned the dog emotionally, just as he expected, but what he had conditioned the dog to understand was futility of trying to escape the shock, of trying to escape "his lot in life." Seligman's lesson objective was to teach the dog to transfer his fear from an object to a sound; what he had actually taught the dog was that he was helpless.

Like so many of us, we go along and form habits of seeing ourselves. We don a mask, as Orwell has written, and live and die behind the fantasy that this mask is who we are. We think, *This is me; this is who I am; this is the me I am stuck with.* We learn to accept what life has to offer with the grim placidity of a condemned prisoner heading to the gallows: we are in chains, and we are unable to change. Just like our four-legged friend, we have learned to be helpless! Listen to the language of learned helplessness in school:

- I am stupid.
- I'm not good in math (or English or Phys. Ed.).
- I'm unlucky; it was Friday the thirteenth.
- The teacher is prejudiced (mean, stinky, an idiot).
- The teacher grades too hard.
- I was feeling ill that day.
- The teacher gave an especially hard test this time.
- I didn't have time to study.
- My wife doesn't understand me. (Okay, this one you'll probably only hear in the teacher's lounge.)

Worst of all, once conditioned to being helpless, even victories, like passing a test or scoring the goal or getting whatever that thing is that you want, becomes at least somewhat Pyrrhic. *How did I do it? I lucked out!*

The habit of helplessness, however, is not necessarily the habit of failure. The colloquial expression noting that even a stopped (analog) clock is right at least twice a day seems somewhat apt here. Helplessness is more the habit of not having any control over the direction of one's life: all events proceed on the power of others, and "fortune" drives life.

Yet even when you are in control of your life, how much power do you have over the flow of existence? "Life just is," said Jerry Brown, governor of California (as of 2013), "it just flows. Go with it." So how are we to see self-control and self-regulation in the storm of life events that visit us regularly and often? Here is the simple, honest truth about success skills: *developing success skills guarantees nothing except that you will have these skills.*

Sorry. That's it. That's the only guarantee you get.

However, having such skills is still very powerful stuff. While it may not be powerful enough to alter the power of an overwhelming adversary, such as the IRS or a terminal illness (is that redundant?), what we can teach, and what we can understand for ourselves, is that it is still quite powerful indeed.

THE BAD NEWS IS TIME FLIES; THE GOOD NEWS IS YOU'RE THE PILOT (MICHAEL ALTHSULER)

It would seem absolutely without question that if one can be conditioned to quit, one can also be conditioned to persevere. If one can learn helplessness, one can also learn powerfulness. It begins with the recognition of what we can control, what we cannot control, and the wisdom to be able to focus energy and drive on those things on which one can have some effect.

While wanting to avoid establishing blame, acceptance of some responsibility still seems to be a key component of being able to begin to internalize and apply critical success skills. Essentially, any change-oriented activity begins, at least on some level, with the recognition that whatever has happened to you, while it may not be entirely your fault, is at the very least partly rooted in something you did. This does not need to be identified as "bad." As Jerry Brown might say, it just is. It is neither good nor bad.

No matter where you are, good, bad, or in between, you have to accept the simple responsibility that you *have* made specific decisions (or worse, have allowed decisions to be made for you) that have carried you along to the very place in which you are right this very minute. Certainly a billion factors, over most of which we have little, if any control, can elevate us to the heights of delirious success or bring us to our knees. At the end of the day all this does is elucidate just how critical it is to apply meaningful intention to those decisions and factors over which we can exert control. Poet Alan Dugan's emotionally complex poem "Love Song: I and Thou" uses the metaphor of house-building as an expression of life. He writes: "This is hell, but I planned it, I sawed it, I nailed it and I will live in it until it kills me."

We all build our own lives, one way or another. But where Dugan's narrator, at least in this very simplified reading, accepts this fate as incontrovertible, perhaps even ironically desirable, the narrator in Portia Nelson's poem is ready to shed her helplessness.

Accepting responsibility for her fate, she is able to focus her energies on getting out of the hole more quickly. Indeed, the narrator begins to practice, apply, and ultimately internalize the kind of self-regulatory, vision-driven thinking that is the critical infrastructure to any series of self-empowered, success-oriented decisions. Her powerfulness even makes her wise.

Although still on the same street, she recognizes the habit now of falling into the same hole, and manages to walk around the danger. She has become, where she can become, proactive in the decisions about her own life and at least, in part because of that, in her final short chapter, she can choose to *walk down a different street*.

IF WE KEEP DOING THINGS THE SAME WAY, AND THEY KEEP NOT LEARNING, WHICH ONE OF US IS THE SLOW LEARNER?

In trying to infuse a family structure in schools that wisely and slowly empower children, it is highly important that decision-making be neither practiced nor taught in an ethical or moral vacuum. However, these ethical and moral structures need to be facilitatively, not judgmentally, determined. Do not underestimate the importance and complexity of such a task.

In trying to create a like way to teach decision-making habits in school, rather than removing ethics and morals from the process, what we want to try to do is diminish the judgmental power of any person's individual ethical or moral beliefs. Ought there be judgments? Yes, of course, but rather they need to take a more subtle, self-directed form rather than be driven by the values of the teacher alone. Telling a student that he has lost your respect may be powerful, but it rarely engenders meaningful change. Consider the judgmental pronouncement in this exchange between this cooperating special education teacher and the student to whom she was assigned in a mainstream class.

Now foolishly this student tried to pass off last year's out-of-class reading as this year's out-of-class reading. When it was discovered, this special education employee (very hard to refer to her as a teacher) decided that the best way to teach this child was to belittle him. "Cheater," she called him, making sure it was loud enough for the whole class to hear. Each time he tried to talk to her she called him a cheater again, and then, just for good measure, she called him a cheater another couple of times as she passed by his desk.

Although this student was often willing to accept responsibility for his mistakes, the belittling exchange left him filled with rage and resentment and closed off to any discussion. It took several extended conversations by a compassionate party at that point to even begin to get him to accept his responsibility.

At first, he roundly claimed that nothing was explicitly stated that precluded his being able to use the book over again, but through discussion, he soon admitted that he understood the spirit of the rule and, soon after, accepted that he had tried a shortcut and was wrong to have done so. Eventually he accepted that he had erred and the accepted consequence of reading another book and completing a new assignment, albeit for a lower grade.

Sadly this righteous missionary zeal that public humiliation will engender better behaviors happens not just at school, but also at work, with friends, and in relationships. As a preventative measure it essentially works no better than do suspensions or prison and, like the latter two, is used simply because the educator or parent knows no other alternative. What such public conflicts create most often is a locked-up intransigence where failing, getting suspended, or even being arrested becomes a better alternative than the "shame" of "giving in."

Fortunately this child had a reasonable party in his life that helped ameliorate the rage he was locked into engendered by the teacher's humiliation. And eventually he accepted both his responsibility and his consequences. He was even able to bring himself to apologize to the regular classroom teacher, though he adamantly refused to apologize to the other teacher regardless of the consequences.

A teacher, trained to foster student self-empowerment, might have turned such an opportunity into a teachable moment, rather than using it as an opportunity to disgorge her self-righteous judgments. Compare that to this exchange over a very similar situation where the teacher, instead of judging the student, invited the student into a conversation to measure himself.

"If you had the choice to have my respect or not have my respect, which would you want?" the teacher asked after she had discovered the student had plagiarized an essay.

"I don't really care. It don't matter to me what you think of me."

"So say if someone wanted to know what I thought of you, it would be alright if I said you were not trustworthy?"

"Well, no, that's not okay."

"So you'd rather have me say, 'Hey, great kid . . . hard worker . . . totally honest.'"

"Well, yeah, sure."

"So, based on your behaviors with the essay and after, how do you think I see you?"

Here is the teachable moment! Here is the facilitative guidance. Here is the opportunity for the student to be able to experience the relationship between decisions and outcomes. People feel about you a certain way sometimes *because* of things that you do. Most people, especially kids, usually would want to be seen in a decent light. When you see how you are assessed as related to actions that are within your control, it opens the door for self-discovery rather than disparagement, which usually forces protectively shutting the door.

Asking a student how he or she might like to be seen by you has essentially the same effect as telling the student how you feel about him or her, but the result is entirely different. In this not-so-subtle shift, students understand your reactions as a consequence of their own actions rather than as a reflection of your feelings alone. Moreover, harsher self-judgment (although it is not really better than harsh external judgment) is a bit easier to accept. When a student makes the connections between a choice that he or she has made, and how he or she is viewed, that student is more likely to understand the connection between personal decision and life outcomes.

There is a wonderful Native American parable, ascribed to the Cherokee, that can be well used as a meme throughout a school or district to bring this idea home to students of any age. The story concerns an elder helping his grandson deal with the child's anger toward a friend.

"Inside people," says the grandfather, "are two wolves in constant battle. One lives on anger, envy, jealousy, greed, arrogance, resentment, inferiority, and false pride; the other lives on peace, love, hope, forgiveness, humility, kindness, generosity, truth, compassion, and empathy."

"Which wolf will win?" the grandson asked.

"That answer is simple," the grandfather replied, "The wolf that will win is the one that you feed."

It's not much more complicated than this: successful people tend to understand this, and see the locus of control for their lives as being within themselves; the less successful you feel, the more likely you are to see the locus of control for your life as being outside yourself. This locus of control is also the difference between being a dependent and an independent learner. Virtually every mission statement in every school district in the United States has as one of its key elements helping students become independent learners. This is one way of getting there.

Consider this quote by John Dewey in respect of the aforementioned differences between interactions: "The teacher is not in the school to impose certain ideas or to form certain habits in the child, but is there as a member of the community to select the influences which shall affect the child and to assist him in properly responding to these influences. The teacher's business is simply to determine, on the basis of larger experience and riper wisdom, how the discipline of life shall come to the child."

Self-definition is crucial, and is the key at any age to being able to marshal any personal resources into a cohesive series of decisions that lead to a personal vision of success. That is why it is critical to create an environment of planning, acting, and objective reflection, which is, actually, the simple heart of this program. Really, that's all it takes:

- plan;
- act;
- reflect;
- make a new plan.

To see the effect of such simplicity on early training, look again at *Tools of the Mind*, which couples constructivist learning concepts with a broad program of self-directed and self-regulatory behavioral learning. In a play-centered learning environment, rather than through a rigid system of compliance and consequences, constant decisions are made by students. Through reflection on these choices, they are taught the basics of how to make wise decisions, and the lessons of having made these decisions are discussed as results rather than consequences.

Initially, not through punitive methods but through the gradual growth of self-knowledge, having students become observers and regulators of their own behaviors is the most important objective. Humiliation is essentially eliminated from miscalculations and mistakes. Indeed, poor choices and the like are seen as amazing opportunities for reflection rather than opportunities for the self-satisfying disgorging of judgmental bile, as characterized previously. Even games are considered opportunities to explore self-knowledge. Take a simple game like musical chairs.

In an average classroom such a game would be played primarily for entertainment, and perhaps as a means to teach students to be graceful winners and good losers, in and of itself not a bad aim. The "winners" would win and the "losers" would sit. In playing the game again, most likely, many of the same kids in the running for victory the time before will be in the running to win again. The certain children who will win at this game more often than others will be characterized as winners, and accorded all the honors and rewards that are "deserved" by these "gifted" kids. The rest of the kids, supposedly, will get to hear a variation of what George Carlin referred to as the most powerful character-building statement of all time ("Billy, you are a loser!"), though it will be embedded in such innocuous statements as "you did just great," "great effort," and "you'll get 'em next time."

Learning to be accepting is not a bad outcome, but there are other options, particularly as a school, that need not decrease the pure fun and joy of play. Instead of only teaching students how to accept their fate and how to live within the status quo, we can instead empower our students to forge radical new paths.

"It is because modern education is so seldom inspired by a great hope," said Bertrand Russell, "that it so seldom achieves great results. The wish to preserve the past rather than the hope of creating the future dominates the minds of those who control the teaching of the young."

Fortunately *Tools of the Mind* teachers embrace the idea that outcomes often have a direct relationship between making a pattern of choices and learning a set of skills. In this program play is important, and grace is also a critical trait to be learned, but they also see that musical chairs, like any other activity, requires specific knowledge and a particular set of abilities that can be acquired (at least to some extent) by any individual motivated enough to learn them to alter the outcome of the game.

What you can do, in playing musical chairs, instead of just playing it the same way again and again and again, is that you can also choose to use it as an opportunity to identify these skills and abilities necessary for winning such a game and start developing them in the students. When a student can identify a specific skill and measure his or her progress along the proficiency continuum of that skill, the praise contained in "good job, Marianna," especially when it identifies some specific action the child undertook to make that progress, does actually become meaningful and does not translate in the student's brain to "Marianna, you are a loser."

It certainly is true that some people are born with certain "gifts" and have perhaps a greater inclination to excel at certain things, like ballet or musical chairs. However, surely anyone powerfully dedicated enough to the task of winning at musical chairs can work on and increase the specific skill set that would allow one to at least improve one's performance.

If you separate out the collection of skills and knowledge exhibited in an average, everyday game of musical chairs, you discover a compendium of skills—such as planning, strategy, multi-tasking, spatial relationships, and more—that can be developed and that are useful even if taken out of the context of the game. And if a person has a passion to learn these skills, in order to do so they also must apply, practice, and internalize the skills of self-regulation, persistence, time management, and so forth, that are critically necessary to learn the other skills, as well as also support musical-chair excellence.

A key understanding about learning success skills is that their importance is most often (but not always) learned when a student is engaged in pursuits of personal meaning that excite their imaginations and/or their passions. It's irrelevant whether they are involved in calculus, coin collecting, or car repair. As long as the student's progress is driven by the desire to learn or excel, significant, deep, and critical learning is happening. It is important that teachers and coaches help facilitate transferring success skills learned though, say, a passion for the computer lab, where the application comes easily, to the writing lab, where it may be more of a struggle.

Persistence developed and applied in the pursuit of passion can be applied to subject areas less driven by desire. The persistence a student marshals to remember and apply highly intricate strategic patterns on the gridiron is exactly the same persistence that can be used to remember and apply complex math functions. Don't assume a student can simply make the transfer, but do assume that the vast majority of students, properly coached, can learn how the strength can be transferred. Many high school coaches, counselors, and educators have counseled a zillion high school athletes to use these same skills to get better grades and open doors for better scholarships, but few have actually facilitated a student's incremental effort to do just that: identify how persistence functions well elsewhere and move it stick by stick to a new location.

A highly successful college football coach, now coaching on the NFL, understood the need for coaches to be teachers first. He made sure that all of his staff understood how to translate information gleaned from players' academic traits and IEPs into ways of helping players become better students of the game. Similarly, the same thinking helped coaches and support staff get players to turn the "success skills" they learned playing the game into one of the top-ten graduation rates in the NCAA.

Again and again, our role as educators is not to judge student desires but rather to help them define their own desires, help them see what they need to learn to get there, and then help them do it. Football coach George Allen rightly noted that "people of mediocre ability sometimes achieve outstanding success because they don't know when to quit."

Students can try and should try, for as long as they are motivated to do so, whatever it is that they are motivated to do. Our job, as developmental educators, is to give students the opportunity to self-assess their personal growth toward some goal against objectified standards. *How deep is this child's passion for musical chairs?* is what we should be asking ourselves, not if this child has the stuff to become a world-class *musical chairist*. Who knows, and what does it matter? Just look at the skills these students are acquiring learning how to become better musical chairs players! Simply put, as much as some of these judgmental, self-important teacher-clerks would like to think it is their job to winnow out from the masses the chosen, golden few, *it just isn't*.

Consider a professor's response to an MBA thesis at Yale. The assignment was to create a proposal for a business that could actually be started, and had some realistic possibility of succeeding. Since it had to be rooted in possibility, this student's grade was a "C." Although well-reasoned, researched, and written, the professor adduced that the idea did not meet the *possibility* requirement and so was deemed less than stellar. What is ironic is that the thesis, written by Fred Smith, was actually the plan he used to start a business he called FedEx (Federal Express). Gross sales in 2012, a slightly down year, topped $40 billion. Yes: *billion*.

As writer Frank Richards points out, "All big things in this world are done by people who are naive and have no idea that is obviously impossible." Success skills can be learned in a chemistry class by a student of very modest scientific abilities and limited professional potential just as well as, and sometimes better than, someone with greater gifts. Sometimes it is the drive to excellence itself that propels them to develop deeper skills and a richer understanding of craft that undergirds future success. If that person has thin talents for the journey, as long as the success skills can be transferred from those learning circumstances to other circumstances if necessary, and they often are, so what? Countless numbers of people have found success on a new path after an abortive foray on a different path, and just as many have waltzed into success in the very areas they were told they would never be good enough.

"You have to try and fail," comedian Louis C. K. says, because "failure gets you closer to what you're good at." What the critical skills program offers, and clearly what programs like *Tools of the Mind* intend to teach, is that learning is a process made up of twists and turns, bumps and bruises, huge leaps and foot slips that above all else decriminalize failure. In fact, *failing doesn't technically become failure until we quit*: until then, it's just process. And process is what learning, learning anything, is all about.

This radical shift of being a process facilitator rather than a judge doesn't even sound so radical. Indeed it merely sounds a lot like good teaching and good learning—doesn't it?

To be great educator, on any level, you must possess the capacity to believe, in the words of Mel Riddile, that "student achievement is not about a student's ability to learn, but rather it is about our ability to teach them." If you believe that statement, and believe in the infinite capacity for human change, then to truly be a teacher you must, absolutely must, accept the capacity that you must be that someone who can help students find a way to open the door for themselves, through which they can then walk.

SMOOTH SEAS DO NOT MAKE SKILLFUL SAILORS (AFRICAN PROVERB)

If helplessness can be learned, confidence can be learned also. However, there are some subtle differences between the way we learn confidence and the way we learn helplessness. Pondering the growth and maturation theories of Erik Erikson's developmental stages, it seems at least somewhat clear that by the toddler stage, the concept of autonomy versus shame and doubt are already formed.

So, in effect, concepts of autonomy and one's ability to have an impact on one's own life are already in place before the first day of school. Still, at that age few children have a clear, deeply formed self-concept, but certainly a child who has gotten the message that he is not smart enough outside of school receiving a similar message in school is at greater risk to believe it fully than a child who gets mixed or positive messages. The problem is that "not smart enough" is often communicated through much more subtle, nonverbal means than merely being demeaned with such an incendiary word as being called "stupid" or an "idiot." Similarly, if the message is "you're helpless," likewise she or he will come to see herself or himself as helpless.

To change, though, from an already-formed self-concept, the nonverbal, nonlanguage components of concept formation are made virtually moot. Once a concept is formed, the child's or adult's experiences are simply emotionally and intellectually reformed to fit the concept. In effect, like any other "virus," a self-concept seeks to protect its own existence. Anyone who sees himself or herself as intellectually inferior will have an extremely hard time seeing any success as having emanated from his or her own intellectual power.

Here are a few ways that the subtle language of "you're not smart enough" gets communicated in school (all of which we've done under the aegis of being motivating):

- One teacher always handed back tests and papers by score: the highest get theirs first.
- An administrator separated a small group of students from the others in a class, telling them they didn't need to listen to him as they were doing just fine academically.
- The "honors" assembly where the entire school goes to the auditorium to watch the students who made it to the honor roll get recognition.

There are even teachers that announce grades aloud, or at least they used to before this became (and rightly so) an invasion-of-privacy issue. Now those teachers just grumble about how this great motivational device is no longer allowed because these soft-on-kids "liberal intellectuals" took over the schools. The issue is not with achievement or success being rewarded; both ought to always be celebrated. But success and achievement are not always based on final outcomes alone, particularly in the learning environment of school. The irony is that most of the students on the "honor roll" have always been on the honor roll and, while they achieve, they may not be showing the level of dedication and improvement exemplified by a student who goes from a 70 percent to an 84 percent, though the latter did not "succeed" at making the honor roll.

The real issue is that choosing what kind of success we reward, and what level of success we reward, especially if we are excluding others from such acknowledgment, creates a division between success and failure rather than fostering a continuum. Students (and even adults) who have failed classes and tests, or anything else for that matter, do not need to be reminded they messed up: they already know. What they do need to know is how to do things differently. What students need from educators is to be able to celebrate success defined in their progress and how to be able to recognize the strengths and intelligences that already exist within them, and apparently, so do many of the professionals in the schools as well.

Vygotsky asserted that thought development, particularly in older youths and adults, is determined primarily by language, both receptive and expressive. This is a marked difference when compared to the linguistic/intellectual capabilities that children have at the toddler stage. The ability to simply believe at the level of naiveté in children creates ripe ground for deeply experienced and ingrained self-concept formation. As discussed earlier, in the nature of habit formation and habit change, it is difficult, and maybe simply impossible, to fundamentally change a habit or concept once formed and deeply experienced. Change becomes a matter of intellectual force, at least initially, rather than simple emotional or automated response.

Tying together both language and concept formation, what one is told, as well as what we tell ourselves, creates a new paradigm that can lead to self-concept (re)formation, which, for the most part, is what we are after. However, it is critical to understand that all of this language-based self-understanding intended to develop a new concept formation must be supported intellectually through metacognition, and by connecting that cognition to actual measures of success, however small. It is this deep understanding that actually helps children, in fact all of us, realize real change, first in behaviors, but ultimately in depth.

Students can learn confidence by employing multiple strategies and multiple efforts solving problems. Students can learn confidence by connecting measurable outcomes to actual actions they took. Students can learn confidence by explaining answers and using metacognition. Learned confidence occurs when teachers, parents, and mentors allow students a measure of frustration and anxiety, in a safe and nurturing environment, while internalizing the idea that failure only becomes failure if they (or we) quit! *The process is the product!*

It takes guts, even more than patience, to help kids take the wheel rather than steer for them. Writer John Holt implored educators to simply "trust children." Yet he acknowledged that nothing could be more difficult because "to trust children we must first learn to trust ourselves, and most of us were taught as children that we could not be trusted." However, understanding the difficulty will help us in our own process of building the confidence to do it. This does not have to be cumbersome. Following chapters will demonstrate how it can be infused into planning and practice in ways that will require few extra hours or simple planning structures.

As professionals we can also exemplify how, when something doesn't work (like suspensions!), we can take what we have learned and create something that works better instead of always doing the same thing "harder." What works better is to help kids *acquire the tools* to do better before challenging them to do better. What works better is encouraging students to take calculated risks and mentoring them through the process of achievement. What works better is using metacognition to help students begin to see the possibility of becoming a different self.

A frequent response teachers get from students who answer a difficult question well, particularly from students who are still evolving (that is struggling to achieve consistently), is almost always "I guessed." Rewarding success can be as simple as refusing to accept a student's explanation for an outstanding answer as a guess. People often make the most compelling leaps of intelligence and imagination under the guise of having guessed! This one teacher responded to a student's "guess" explanation by saying he didn't believe in guessing.

"But it was a guess," said the student. "Trust me."

"You know what I think? I think something happened in that brain of yours, and I think that it happened so fluidly, and so rapidly, that you were not even aware."

The teacher started asking a series of questions, moving backward from the answer: What were you thinking just before the answer jumped in? What popped into his head when the question was first asked? In the space of a few simple questions, the student began to grasp that what he had come up with was not a guess, but an answer that so rapidly connected ideas he had been collecting before the question stimulated his response that he didn't even notice it.

"Do you still believe you guessed at the answer?"

"No," he said, a bit sheepishly but also with just a smidgen of pride.

"Just remember," the teacher whispered, loud enough for the class to hear, "you're now in my secret scholars club. Don't worry, though, I won't tell anybody how smart you are."

The entire exchange just described took perhaps three minutes, but in the end it was not just a lesson in thinking for the student whose brain was examined; it was also a lesson for the whole class that thinking is not an accident. It is not a walk across the stage to receive a victory medal of scholastic honor, to be sure, but a single step is as big a victory to some as a record-breaking leap is to another. Consider rewarding both of those at an honors assembly and maybe we will all be finally on the right path.

FIVE

A Simple Prescription for Self-Regulation and Decision-Making

Take These Frequently, Every Day

> We are what we repeatedly do. Excellence, therefore, is not an act but a habit. —Aristotle

Here's what critical success skills come down to: self-regulation, decision-making, organization, time management, persistence, and, at a bare minimum, *workplace* social skills (regarding students' school-as-work-related social skills—specifically, how students interact with adults and in the presence of adults). These are the core critical success skills. Develop them, and you might succeed. Don't? Well here is that dirty little secret again: even if you don't apply critical success skills you might well succeed anyway.

It would be great to proffer an incontrovertible truth, driven by data gleaned from a double blind study, that the acquisition, practice, and internalization of these skills could guarantee you will live the life you have imagined, but the truth, as Thomas of Occam asserted, is often much simpler than that.

This book makes one single assertion: if you learn to apply critical success skills, you will be assured that you will have the capacity to apply critical success skills. To promise anything else would simply be false. The writer Jean Cocteau would agree. "Of course I believe in luck," he once said. "How otherwise to explain the success of some people you detest?"

The newspapers are of full of stories of ne'er do wells who get bailed out of every imbroglio into which their lack of planning and willful disregard for consequences put them. Their great luck was to be born to parents with the capacity to make bail. And there are, as well, people who have done everything wrong and still wound up sitting on the terrace of an oceanfront condo on a pile of dough just because they happened to be at the right place at the right time when it fell from the sky.

At the same time there is little doubt that people who have some ability to apply these skills report a greater sense of control over their lives, a greater amount of satisfaction with their lives, and if in fact they do not have *everything* that they want, as few ever do, they have much of what they need to be content. "We almost always have choices," notes psychologist William Glasser, "and the better the choice, the more we will be in control of our lives."

The simple truth is that some of the wealthiest people in the world are high school dropouts, but also so are some of the poorest. However, one would assume, as a percentage, there are fewer dropouts who achieve the success of a Richard Branson than those who wind up sweating the rent every month. As teachers, therefore, we ought to be equipping our students not with a map to find buried treasure, but rather with something a little more akin to what Ernest Hemingway referred to as the writer's most essential tool: "a built in, shock proof sh*t detector."

The core of these critical success skills is really *decision-making* (self-regulation, also a core critical skill, usually exists in the world of solid decision-making). First and foremost, the ability to make consistently high-quality, meaningful decisions is the beginning habit of a success-oriented life. It is also the key to building successful classrooms, successful schools, and successful students. Before you can become a great student, you must decide that a great student is what you want to be. This is the key ethos that must move to the center of a school's instructional mission.

In doing so we can give our students, and perhaps even ourselves, a simple tool for envisioning the future, creating a strategic plan to get there, and finally a means by which you can assess progress and, when necessary, alter decisions to produce outcomes more in line with real desires. In doing this we give our students, and maybe even ourselves, a chance to create a measure of control in an otherwise-chaotic universe. It is simpler to do than most people imagine: the hard part is creating good decision-making as a habit.

The beginning for a school community is to select simple code words, repeated often and applied consistently throughout a school or even a district. These code words define the process of decision-making in a simple, straightforward, effective way and can go a long way toward creating the fertile ground for understanding what needs to be done so that the seeds of habit can take root.

Plan, act, and reflect is one code set. *Dream, do, deduce* could be another. The key to any decision-making plan is to be able to decide what you want, or where you want to go, create the plan, execute the plan, reflect on the outcomes of that execution, and then create a new plan adjusted by this knowledge. It is a constant and constantly repeated cycle. How we name this process is really irrelevant as long as, just as in a family, we are using this common vocabulary to create consistent and clear practices.

A very effective one, as proffered in the Michael Pritchard documentary called the *Power of Choice* (I think this verbiage seems to appeal to students) is the code: *VIP*. (For demonstration purposes these terms will be used, but any word pattern consistently applied can be just as effective.)

Now Pritchard tells kids that *VIP* normally stands for Very Important Person. In the *Power of Choice* video he tells them, "You are a *very* important person." Indeed, each and every one of us is the single most important person in our lives if for no other reason than the simple fact that in the entire world, in the whole of the universe (in the multi-verse in fact!) there is only one single thing we can control and that is our own personal decisions.

Think about this: how many decisions do you think you make in the course of a day? Ask students, even adults, to answer this question and you'd get amazingly diverse responses. Some people think they make three or four decisions a day; others see the numbers in the trillions. The truth is few researchers seem to be able to state with any accuracy just how many decisions we make in the course of a day, let alone agree on exactly what a decision constitutes.

There is so much automaticity in decision-making that very often an actual decision may be mistaken for an involuntary response, but even the most conservative estimates seem to indicate that the numbers of decisions any human being makes in the course of a day is countless. This paragraph alone, which contains one hundred words or so, involves minimally 499 decisions just to select the letters! And that's even before we start talking about spaces, punctuation, and the *pondering* that has resulted in choosing these specific words, in this specific order, to mean whatever in the end it all means.

The numbers do not matter: the important question is not how many decisions one makes, but which of these decisions are truly important. In reality, though, we can only guess, and never really know, which decision is going to be important and which not. In John Boorman's wonderful film *Excaliber* the wizard Merlin makes a statement that is an excellent definition of how we determine the importance of decisions we make.

Young King Arthur, smitten by Guinevere, ponders the stirring of his feelings for her while he eats a small cake she has made intended to help him heal from his battle wounds. Merlin points out that life and love are very much like the cake he is about to eat. "You never know what life is about until you bite into it," says Merlin, "and then, of course, it is too late."

So how are we to counsel our students, our children, and even ourselves to live if every decision we make is just another fling into a chaotic universe? Here again, is Pritchard's simple answer: *VIP: Vision, Initiative, and Perspective.*

VISION

> If you don't know where you're going, you'll probably never get there.
> —Anonymous

Before you can be anything, before you can do anything, before you can put one foot in front of the other, you have to decide. Probably the only things that aren't a decision, on a personal level, are breathing, blood flow, and organ functions. Even such prosaic activities as defecating and urinating are decisions, at least until they're not. Everyone at some point or another has made the choice to "hold it."

Decisions define our days, but decisions regarding our vision for ourselves define our lives. There is a great aphorism attributed to supermarket magnate Frank Outlaw. He says, "Your thoughts become your words, your words become your actions, your actions become your habits, you habits become your character, and your character becomes your destiny." It's a powerful idea but one that is frequently overlooked by those who, as Thoreau might have said, choose not to live deliberately. This is not to say that people cannot differ on the level of deliberateness.

There are some who are more goal oriented, who may not be able to take step one on a spring afternoon walk until they have a specific destination. Another person more comfortable with a different level of spontaneity might not need to have a clear plan to start moving. The key is knowing what it is that you need, and to be clear that, even if you are a person to whom open highways are more alluring, you are actually going somewhere and not just drifting down the roads of daily life.

That is *vision*.

Sometimes decisions are not driven at all by "performance" or "destination" outcomes. They are driven instead by perceptual ideas, character ideals, and concepts of right and wrong. Someone may say, for instance, "I don't care where I wind up, or what my financial future turns out to be, so long as in the end I can say that I acted as a person of integrity and was an honest person." This ideal is just as much a "destination" as the journey to opening the door to the CEO's office that has just been adorned with the letters of your name. These, too, drive the day-to-day and moment-to-moment decisions we must make. Vision then is (among a zillion other possibilities):

- creating a picture of an outcome;
- setting a specific and attainable goal;

- seeing yourself as something or someone you can become;
- creating an ethical ideal.

Vision is the dream stage, and in some ways, the easiest part of the process. Who doesn't want to live a beautiful dream? But to be a manageable vision, you must have some specificity. I want to be rich; I want to be in the NFL; I want a good grade. These may seem somewhat specific, but in fact they are probably not specific enough.

Specificity does several critical things. Chief among them is the specific almost automatically formulates realism, and this realism often forges not just the need but also the *ability* to create a strategic plan. The straightforward "I want a B this year in biology class" or the "I want to be an internet start-up millionaire by the time I'm thirty" almost always trumps the much more amorphous "I want a good grade; I want to be rich" idea. The next section will explore why specificity has that power, but for now, let's just say that having a specific vision is like making a down payment on something you are trying to buy: a down payment doesn't ensure anything except that the purchaser is probably serious and therefore more likely to follow through.

A great example of the critical importance of having a clear vision was offered by a former drug addict during a school visit. In respect of teaching critical skills, these sorts of "I screwed up" lectures offer little of worth, though the stories are often memorable and moving. In lectures provided by family court judges, police, junkies, former gang members, prisoners and ex-prisoners, and even groups of actors performing plays about prison, avoiding gangs, or not becoming an alcoholic/addict, the story is frequently the same: look at what I did, how bad it got, so don't do it!

Again, it is all well meaning, and may actually reach the few kids who are more motivated, say, by the fear of prison than the power of a positive notion. Most already know they don't want to go to prison just as they know they don't want to be junkies or to be in trouble in school. What students don't understand, and what few of these programs provide, is how to behave differently now so that you don't have to go to rehab in the first place! Such "learning entertainments" might serve students better if they feature people who have used positive decision-making to avoid becoming crackheads in the first place.

Does anyone think that if a kid could behave differently, and not be in trouble all of the time, she would? *Does anyone want to grow up to be an alcoholic?*

However, this former addict did address the issue of his own addiction in a way, at least for those who were listening (this may be a huge shock, but kids aren't really attentive in these meetings), that gave some powerful insight into how he became an addict, and how he might have actually avoided such a fate.

He told the students that twenty years ago he was, like them, a high school senior sitting in exactly the same kind of place. He remembered clearly, he said, a man just like he was today, talking to the students and telling his story of getting messed up on drugs. The speaker, a slender, soft-spoken, middle-aged fellow, remembered that he had even said aloud at that very lecture that this story they had just heard would never ever be his story. He said he just knew that was never going to be addicted to drugs because, up until then, he had never even had a sip of alcohol, let alone a drug, in spite of the fact that there had been plenty of opportunity. So, he asked the kids, "You are probably wondering, how did I get here?"

"Any of you kids ever see that United Negro College fund commercial?" he asked. "You know the one where the interviewer goes up to a bunch of Black children who are graduating from high school and they ask these kids, 'What are your plans for after graduation?' One kid says he's going to Howard; another kid says he's going to a local state university, another kid says he's going to Princeton; and finally they go up to this one kid and they say to him, 'What are you doing after graduation?' and he says, 'You know, I think I'm just going to go home and get myself a sandwich.' Then of course the tagline is 'A mind is a terrible thing to waste.' Well, folks, although I wasn't in that commercial, that character in that commercial? That was me."

He talked about how he really had no plans beyond graduating high school, no goals, but even so his addictions did not happen all of a sudden. It wasn't like he woke up one day and made a decision to be a drug addict. In fact, it would even be a couple of more years until he finally started to succumb at all, but it is an important factor to note that those were a couple of years of vague, unfocused planning pervaded by a sense that he was not really going anywhere. Although he had a couple of jobs in a couple of places, he was without an aim, without a purpose, and there was just too much sitting around, too much TV, and too much of nothing.

Somewhere around twenty, he recalled, he was hanging out with a few friends who were drinking and seemed to be having a better time than he was. So he had a drink or two with these buddies he'd been hanging out with, and since that felt pretty good, he had some more. Several months later he thought, *Oh what the hell.* Everybody else he had been hanging out with was getting high and having a good time, so he might as well too, and that felt even better. And then, after a while, he thought, *Hey, a bunch of the others I'm running with are using, so I might as well try skin popping a little as well.* "And the next thing you know," he said, "it's ten, twelve years later and for most of that time, you've been a bust-out junkie."

This was so much the opposite of how drugs and drug addiction is characterized, at least at the school level. It accounts, at least in part, for the ineffectiveness of DARE-type programs. The message usually is once you know how awful and disgusting drugs are, and the abject misery of addiction, you will never, never, never, never, never touch the stuff. And that usually works, until someone you think of as being cool actually offers you some at party and a couple of hits later you're thinking all that crap they told you was crap: *this is some good stuff!*

This is not going to be an argument about the rights and wrongs of drinking or using drugs. In general, in fact, most successful people tend to live generally sober lives, or at the very least can limit and control the intake of their pleasures. However, the truth about drugs and alcohol (and chocolate, and empty carbohydrates, and fattening foods, and sex, and just about anything else) is that all these things can be enjoyable, and even fun, but all have addictive aspects, and mere resistance, without a better purpose, is only sometimes successful.

A compelling study of television-watching found little proof that watching any television program, regardless of how inane or sexual or violent it was, had a definitive impact on long-term behaviors. The study revealed that the single clear negative of television-watching, particularly excessive television-watching, was that while watching TV one lost countless hours that might have been spent doing something of greater value, at least in respect of life-enhancing opportunities. Similarly, you can drink all you want to forget your problems, but those same problems are always going to be waiting for you at the bottom of that last drink; it'll just be later.

The bottom line is that the ultimate "negative" about TV (or pretty much anything else, whatever it is), is never going to be stronger than that call of its short-term pleasures. Drugs, alcohol, junk food, TV can appear to induce happiness, but in the end can also be damaging, and not just if they are overused to the point of excess and self-destruction. Time spent inducing a vision is not the same as time spent creating a vision. This idea will be revisited later, but suffice for now to say without a clear and compelling vision for our lives, we are at the mercy of powers unseen, and while we may arrive exactly where we want to be, it will only be the whims of others and not our own strengths that get us there.

Most people, directly asked, students and adults alike, express a desire not to live lives at the mercy of whim and circumstance. Yet until we develop the capacity for planning and following through on such plans, we are at their mercy. Creating a vision, though, is a great start.

INITIATIVE

How we spend our days is, of course, how we spend our lives. —Annie Dillard

Dreaming is great, and it is great fun, because in dreams we all get rock-hard abs by eating cheeseburgers. In reality, though, if you want that trim, sexy core, as they say in the infomercials, you'll have to start by at least shutting off the infomercials.

In his *Paris Review* interview, the great and esteemed writer Bernard Malamud talked about the struggle to write first drafts. "It's where you need the guts," he said, "the ability to live with the imperfect until you can make it better." Anybody who has ever struggled through the "first draft" of anything, and in life of course we are almost always writing our first drafts, knows Malamud is exactly right.

So we dream of stuff we want, and things we want to do, and places we want to be, and lives we want to live, and in each dream there is a spark, often faint, that can be captured. To capture that spark, to nurture that spark, to turn that spark into a fire, to get what you want (here's the infomercial part), really and honestly and guaranteed for life, it works every time, to get anything and everything you have ever wanted, and ever will want (act now before the stuff you want is all gone), all you ever really need to do are *three simple things*:

- Start.
- Get off your butt.
- Do something.

The only catch is that you have to keep on doing it until you get whatever that magic thing is that you want. Actually, this looks suspiciously like real work. While it seems as though this is oversimplifying these activities, they are at their core pretty simple. Why invent complications? Why create a bunch of mindless activities and make a load of mindless forms to fill out (worksheets 1, 2, 3, 4, and 4a) that give teachers, parents, and kids the illusion that they are actually doing something when in fact they are not?

Simply put, here is what initiative is:

- breaking a "grand" vision down into a process of attainable "mini-goals";
- making positive decisions toward accomplishing each goal, objective, or vision of oneself; and
- following through with actions intended to meet those goals.

Seriously, what could be simpler? When confronted with options, as we all are, all the time, just choose the option that seems most likely to take you in a positive direction toward the goal that you want to achieve. Yikes! It doesn't take superhuman powers, or an advanced degree from *Nike* University (or whatever brand-name school everybody wants to get into this week), or even a lot of will power, not at least at the outset (although, to be accurate, will does play a significant part). Yet it is sometimes the simplest, the most obvious that is the hardest to see.

Keep it simple.

So let's say you are conversing with a student who totally messed up her social studies grade last year but still managed to squeak by and finds herself in your next-level class. And let's say further that this student has shared with you a desire to improve her grade this year, understanding, as she does, the impact of grade acquisition on admission to a prestigious college from which she can then leap into the stratosphere of entrepreneurial fame and multimillion-dollar bonuses in the world of work.

Most people, and they would be right, would simply tell the student to do what is required of her throughout the year, and perhaps, wanting the penultimate A+ (without which, *certainly*, such megabuck bonuses would surely be out of reach), do a little extra in the way of schoolwork and studying. While this is right, it is often simply not helpful primarily because it isn't exactly news. Day one of school, at any age, there isn't a child that doesn't know this.

What they also probably already know is that in order to achieve this they are going to have to achieve a few "process goals" along the way to the big-dream payoff. But what they often do not know is what all those "process goals" look like, and how to break down the long-term outcome into these small, accruing parts and then reform all of that process into a long-term outcome through deciding, planning, organizing, self-regulating, and persisting. This is where the teacher who chooses to be facilitative rather than purely directive has a clear advantage.

One skill that a facilitative teacher brings to the interaction, that a directive teacher often does not, is a willingness to remember the "how it was gotten" and not just the "what it is" of an acquired skill. Before a skill (of any sort: think of reading) can be internalized and automated, it must be acquired piecemeal and thoughtfully employed. When we remember the process by which we have acquired *all* of our own skills (some skills are learned more quickly and more easily than others, but the process is always pretty much the same), we instantly become empathic to the need of those who are learning from us who must also acquire these skills in pieces and over a long period of time. Instantly it increases our willingness to coach a child or adult through their own process of learning and employing these skills.

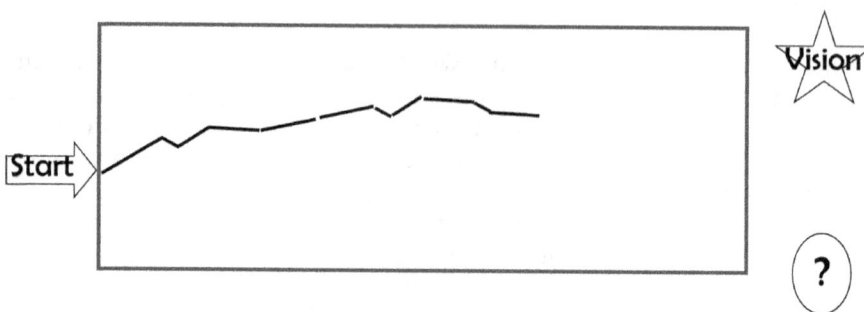

Figure 5.1.

As figure 5.1 illustrates, the setting of a goal or a *vision* can create a standard, a place to go, a destination. For simplicity's sake, think about a destination you had to go to recently, say, to meet a friend at a coffee shop. If you were unsure about how to get there, you would certainly seek the knowledge of how to get there.

The barista could certainly tell you how to get there, if you chose to call, and that would be fine for any "normal" interaction where the end is just getting to the cafe. However, a facilitative teacher, like any good parent, needs to build into their interactions their own obsolescence. By teaching map reading, or how to use digital mapping software, as most teachers would, the student is empowered with the skill to get from the very spot on which they stand to where they want to be later. Every reached destination is then an accomplishment rather than merely an arrival.

When it comes to academics, we would fire any teacher who believed otherwise. Yet, about success skills, a more critical acquisition that creates the foundation to acquire all the other learning, a typical exchange is characterized in this wholly directive interaction from an old burlesque comic routine:

"Hey, Pal, how to do you get to City Hall?"

"Well, Pal, usually I just get in my car and drive there!"

Yet, essentially, this is the kind of advice we give kids every day. How do I do better in school? Do your homework, read more, and watch TV less. How do I make better decisions? You just do what you need to do.

"Hey, Pal, how to do you get to the future?"

"Usually I just get in my digitized personal teleportation conveyance and appear there."

Such exchanges are not facilitative teaching. Simply put, telling students what to do is not teaching them how to do it, and facilitating initiative is at the heart of teaching success skills.

Creating a vision for the future, particularly if that vision is specific and attainable, creates the need for disciplined thinking and strategic planning. Facilitating the movement toward that vision helps children, or whomever you are coaching, become aware of how action "A" today may impact on a desired outcome many days or many miles from the moment of a seemingly inconsequential decision. In effect it separates out the important decision from the other billions and billions of decisions. Since, as Kierkegaard writes, "life must be lived forward but can only be understood backwards," how else would we define important?

As we make them, the important decisions are, in fact, the ones that appear to be important to our future plans as we have defined them. While doing what you need to do may be another story entirely, knowing what you need to do, and especially knowing what you need to do first, and second and third, has to come first.

A perfect, and perfectly powerful, example of how to break down an incredibly difficult task into achievable mini-goals, and then stay the course, was replicated in a movie called *Touching the Void*. This quasi-documentary depicted a fateful Andean Mountain climb by two Englishmen, Joe Simpson and Simon Yates. In brief, the story is that near the apex of this expedition Simpson took a particularly nasty fall, driving his lower leg into his kneecap, and shattered them both.

Yates was forced to try to help Simpson down the mountain after the injury by lowering him stage by stage and with two long climbing ropes knotted together, Simpson trussed at one end and Yates trussed at the other. This meant that at its greatest point Simpson and Yates might be as much as 150 feet apart and, given the terrain, often unable to make a visual connection. They were about halfway down the mountain when, as Yates was lowering Simpson, he felt a sudden drop. He was unable to determine, at such a great distance, Simpson's fate. Yates struggled to hang on hoping that Simpson might stabilize himself, but all he felt was Simpson's weight pulling him closer to the edge.

Yates continued to hold, for several hours, continually tugging at the rope in the hopes of feeling a return tug, their agreed-upon form of distance communication, with the growing fear that he himself might eventually be pulled into whatever abyss Simpson had fallen. Although Yates's efforts were heroic, eventually, when Yates determined that he was at grave risk of being pulled down the mountain himself to save a man who, for all he was able to determine, might have been dead already, he felt he had no choice but to cut the rope and save himself.

Actually Simpson was still alive and dangling over a deep crevasse, but because of the way his own weight held the rope against the ledge, he was neither able to receive nor send the tugging signal. When Yates cut him loose, Simpson (who, by the way, bears no ill will and feels Yates had no other choice in order to save his own life) fell another hundred feet or so, breaking through some ice and winding up further into an ice cave. Though in enormous pain, and barely able to move from his previous injury and from this fall, Simpson knew if he didn't do something, he was dead.

By some good fortune, he eventually noticed light coming from a lower opening than the one he had fallen through, and was able to slowly and painfully crawl through that small opening and out onto some frozen tundra. He found his bearings and worked his way off the glacier onto less dangerous terrain, but he determined he was still several miles away from base camp.

Dehydrated, frost bitten, starving, hobbling on one leg but mostly crawling, Simpson managed to drag himself for several days. Finally he got close enough to the base camp that his weak voice was heard by Yates, who, along with a fellow adventurer, had been reluctant to break camp, hoping, somehow, Simpson might have survived. By the time Simpson arrived at base camp the situation was so dire he had to be airlifted to the hospital.

Now to be sure there were some serendipitous moments of good fortune: the light identifying the lower opening; Yates's unwillingness to give up hope; even that Yates was having difficulty falling asleep on a still, quiet night so that he was actually able to hear Simpson's weak voice calling for help. What was truly incredible, though, was how Simpson, under the kind of life-and-death duress that few are ever forced to handle, managed the arduous, painful journey from his almost-certain death to his survival.

What he found, he said, was that each time he thought of the enormous distance he had to travel, and the prospect of that much pain, he became overwhelmingly frightened, demoralized, and unable to move. However, he also realized that to survive he had no alternative but to travel an almost-impossible distance. What he found was that while he was overwhelmed by the prospect of a whole journey of acute pain, he was able to manage short, intense bursts of that acute pain over a smaller distance.

He would see a tree perhaps one hundred feet away, and he would set his sights on the tree. The level of pain he must have withstood, even over that short distance, seems unimaginable, but certainly the prospect of a managing that level of pain for the fifteen or twenty minutes it might take him to drag himself to the next tree was simply not as overwhelming as imagining the "lifetime" of pain over the entire distance back to camp.

"Perception is strong and sight weak," writes Miyamoto Musashi, considered one of Japan's greatest samurai warriors and military tacticians. He notes that "in strategy, it is important to see distant things as if they were close and take a distanced view of close things."

While we will get into this concept more when we discuss perspective, it is important to be aware that Simpson applied Musashi's strategic dictum probably without even knowing it, but it is the essence of initiative and persistence.

Focusing only on the unendurable pain of the distance of the ultimate destination overwhelmed Simpson's desire to survive and left him unable to move. However, knowing each segmented distance had an endurable duration allowed Simpson to take a "distanced" enough view of the pain to move toward his keen vision of survival in small, more manageable components. While each section must have unbelievably difficult, breaking down the process into small, manageable goals was exactly what he needed in order to persist, and to survive.

These skills exhibited by Simpson, though in extreme dramatic fashion, are those same skills we apply to more mundane but equally important tasks. Making informed decisions is a learned skill; the ability to break down a long process into attainable segments is a learned skill; the ability to be persistent is a learned skill. Most importantly, the ability to live in momentary difficulty in exchange for a better future is a learned one. In any school district there are hundreds, if not thousands, of highly intelligent children who underperform, fail, and even drop out for want of the ability to decide in a way that enhances their future rather than thwarts it.

Facilitating effort must go beyond the typical getting-started phase of much academic work in order to have students learn the fundamentals of initiating and being persistent. Fostering a difficult beginning of something may be all that is needed for those who have already learned how to accelerate, but helping the rest of the kids make a deep, visceral connection of the relationship between even minor accomplishment and movement toward a goal is of consummate importance. This is exactly what initiative is: start, get off your butt, do something, restart. It is also the method by which persistence is created and fostered and built. Persistence is the DNA of success.

Victory rarely comes with thunder and the blare of trumpets. Most often little manageable changes, almost seemingly inconsequential alterations, create startling patterns that become shifts that move us as well as our children in amazing new directions. Great teachers seize on these moments and give them *appropriate* attention.

The key in being facilitative is not so much to reward these accomplishments (however seemingly small) with accolades, though frequent, relevant praise is always a powerful tool, but rather we want to use praise as *guided critical reflection* to help the student see and value what they already are accomplishing.

A student decided to start a fund-raising effort for the victims of a tragic natural disaster. He managed, by himself, to raise almost $300 but considered his effort an abject failure because he had set his sight on a much higher number. Ultimately we want this student to be able to grow to do this for himself, but initially, at least, doesn't it appear that this is a student in need of guidance in order to be able to take a more balanced, objective overview? While such an effort falling short of a goal may not be an "unqualified success," it is critical to help this student connect to what has been successful, for his own self-esteem as well as to be able to build future successes on already-learned acts of success.

The reality is that many of us miss or discount our successes simply because much of it is so diminutive it is almost microscopic. However, when we can find these truths in our own experiences, we can deepen our understanding of our students' and children's struggles by accurately seeing our own. Each success has a critical feature: properly internalized, any even modest victory increases a "fuel supply" that we can draw on when we need that extra *ooomph* to keep on in a tough time.

"I think I can," the famous mantra of the children's book *The Little Engine That Could* might have actually been initially written as:

I think I can; really, I think I can. Okay, I've never actually gone over the big mountain before but I think I can because I have gone over a lot of smaller hills and mountains. They were hard, too, but I remember even the first time I was able to go over a small hill, it was a bit of a strain on my fuel supply but somehow I kept trying. I told myself just fifteen more feet, just ten more feet; you can do that; just keep trying just a little more and suddenly I crested that little hill! I did it! Since I did those other ones, even though this time it will be bigger and harder, I think if I apply the same level of effort for just a little while longer, I think I can get over this one, too. I think I can, because I have. I think I can, because I have. I think I can. I think I can. I think I can!

At least that's how author Watter Piper probably wrote it before his editor said, "Trust me, Watter, if you just write, 'I think I can,' it says the same thing!" And actually, if you truly relate the little engine's experience to your own experience, it does.

Understanding the power of breaking a large and complex task down into smaller attainable goals is not always difficult, but ironically seeing each incremental gain as having merit frequently is. Often young men and women do not equate passing a test, getting a B- in a course, graduating from middle school, high school, or even college as an accomplishment because they are too busy thinking about what they wanted rather than what they did. Teachers and parents also can sometimes demean the very thing that is most powerful: a simple, almost-inconsequential action that opens our minds to a bit of light is as powerful a revelation as the heaven parting if through it we have learned something.

Educators can facilitate this kind of understanding in part by sharing such stories of how some modest success contributed to their own big accomplishments, of which we are rightly proud. *You know, it didn't seem like a lot at the time, but I think when I cut down from three bottles to one bottle of soda a day, it was the beginning of my losing all that weight!*

Most importantly, influential adults can create the foundation for helping students identify and value these (seemingly) inconsequential accomplishments themselves. One example of this was a coach who gave a game ball to a player who got a hit but was left on base when the final out was made the second-to-last inning. The player was shocked.

With two outs he had hit a modest "seeing eye" single that squibbed through the infield and then was left on first when the batter behind him struck out on three straight pitches. However, the next inning, with two outs and a runner on first and second, the team's most consistent hitter got an at bat and slapped the first pitch deep enough that the runner on first was able to score the game-ending run. He got the game ball because without his hit, all things being equal, the game would have been over before the game-winning hit could have been hit.

Each success has value, just like each rep with a weight, each draft of a paper, each science experiment retried, builds strength, grit, temerity, determination, and persistence, all of which plays a part in initiating and maintaining the level of work necessary to achieve at high levels.

Black Elk, the famed "Medicine Man" of the Oglala Lakota (Sioux) nation, said, "Continuous effort, not strength or intelligence, is the key to unlocking our potential." This continuous effort, this persistence, not only can be learned but also must be learned because the potential that we believe is in all of us does not usually bubble up to the surface: it must be mined. What our students need to know is that when it comes to their potential it is their work level that must rise to meet it or their potential will surely shrink down to meet the student's level of effort.

By helping students connect with (appropriate) pride to even small successes, we build their belief in themselves. Referring back to figure 5.1, if you think of each segment of that line as a decision that you made about what you chose to do in a moment, you can see that some of those segments take you toward your goal, and some away. In a word, that's life, and as Frank Sinatra sings: "You're riding high in April, shot down in May, but I know I'm going to change their tune, when I'm back on top, back on top in June."

Each activity, each lesson, each moment is an opportunity to move in a different direction. Yet much of what causes students to dismiss this and quit on themselves and their dreams is not even so much the fear of failure but a belief in the fatality (or finality) of failure. As professional educators and education managers we bear some responsibility for this. Many educators, again, meaning well, do take this fatalistic approach to interacting with students. Opportunity knocks but once! Fail a test: you've blown it! Missed a deadline: you're done!

A simple question: How many times in schools is learning time open-ended?

The answer is, of course, not often, or at least not often enough. William Glasser even noted that there were only "two places in the world where time takes precedence over the job to be done: school and prison."

Issues of management often preclude educators from varying time expectations but, as "near parents," we also have some responsibility to make sure that school is really about learning in the real world and not just learning in school. Learning in the real world has few time specifications. For instance, there are few instances outside of school and government where "timed" tests are taken seriously. There are even fewer instances where tests matter at all, or where deadlines are created without input, when the occasion allows it, from those people responsible for meeting the deadline. Even journalists' deadlines in the internet age have gone the way of . . . well, printed newspapers. Shouldn't we build some of that into school? Why shouldn't young writers, for instance, be allowed continual revisions (within parameters) until such time as the writing and the grade have met expectations?

There is truth that opportunity sometimes comes but once, and making the most of your chance is important. However, just as often the very same opportunity may knock frequently, sometimes even to better effect. It's not hard to find a story where a person, turning down a job offer today, might find himself or herself the recipient of that same job offer several more times, often with increased inducement. Opportunities sometimes come frequently, especially to people with vision and initiative who often create their own opportunities where none previously existed. For them opportunity never knocked at all, but fortunes have been acquired on just such nonopportunities.

Yet in school, we kill initiative by holding to an outmoded idea that opportunity knocks but once and that mistakes are always fatal. Take for instance the principal of a large high school especially proud of her *zero-tolerance toughness*, who asked an assistant principal candidate how she would respond if a graduating senior signed a contract to "behave" for the final twenty days of school in order to *walk* during the ceremony and, after eighteen days with good behavior, gets removed from a class on day nineteen.

The candidate knew full well that even Jethro Bodine (from the Beverly Hillbillies . . . c'mon, it's not that old!) would know that the right answer would have been, "whelp, if'n he signed a contract, I reckon he jus' cain't go to the gradj-ee-ation." For a moment she even toyed with such a response. Yet even knowing that her words would be a rusty razor she was drawing across her own neck, the candidate replied that assuming the infraction was something mild (having perhaps a personal meltdown as opposed to throwing a punch at a teacher), she would not take away a once-in-a-lifetime experience from a student who had shown such considerable progress. It was, of course, the wrong answer.

The principal, who apparently also has a zero-tolerance policy for opinions that differ from hers, ended the interview immediately, insisting that since a contract was a contract, the candidate's lack of willingness to hold the student accountable was a clear indication of her lack of ability to be a school leader. She noted that if they "opened the door" to looking into the nuances of every behavior of every student that came into the office, all they would be doing all day is talking to kids. That, according to this principal, "was insane." And it would be insane to interact with kids all day, unless of course that was your job and the first sentence of the mission statement of that particular school district recognized that "each person has inherent worth" and a right to be treated as an individual.

Setting aside the question of the value of such behavioral contracts, the rigid nature of how this contract would be enforced actually not only belies the reality of contracts (which are renegotiated almost all of the time in one way or another), but also absolutely does not teach what most schools claim to value: learning. How have we taught the value of progress if a single mistake, a single poor decision (again, assuming it was not an egregious error) can eradicate the value of any progress? While this certainly exists in the world, the ethics of any supervisor who would consider only an employee's mistakes and none of his or her successes in an evaluation would be considered, at the very least, suspicious, if not actually specious.

Interacting with students to build their capacity to master their own behavior and decision-making requires active, careful listening and a willingness to act in the best interest of student learning, not just in *school time*, but in *life time*. Such externalized and rigid structures as "zero-tolerance" policies enforced with zero thinking rarely result in the learning of self-interested personal-management skills that produce true and meaningful self-regulation.

Is it more time-consuming to assess value, to weigh nuances, and to engage with students in meaningful self-assessment than to just blindly enforce rules? Of course. Thinking deeply about what is in the best interest of each child and helping a child understand the relationship between personal actions and outcomes may not be the most efficient way to manage children, but it is absolutely how you teach a child to be both self-respecting and respectful of others.

In decision-making, and in teaching initiative, teachers and parents merely need remember that one is always moving in the direction of his or her last decision. Any decision is essentially a living organism, and all living things are always in motion, always subject to change. Reflect on the direction that whatever decision you have made has taken you. Like it? Follow it up with a decision in the same vein. Don't like it? Make a different decision.

Instantly you are moving, however greatly or infinitesimally, in a new direction! This is the essence of initiative and perhaps the only power we have. In the wild and chaotic world, the only thing we can control is us. "You can never go back and make a new start, my friend," writes Carl Bard, "but you can always start from wherever you are and make a brand-new end."

Failure, just like punishment and consequences, does not teach a thing. However, as John Dewey points out, when we reflect on our failures, we can begin to learn. Negative outcomes are instantly transmogrified from failure to mere data that informs the flow of future learning. This is the essence of initiative boiled down to a fine sauce that, when it becomes a core practice of the whole school, teaches simply this idea referred to in the last chapter: *Failure only becomes failure when we quit! Until then, it is just process.*

PERSPECTIVE

> To accomplish great things, we must not only act, but also dream; not only plan, but also believe. —Anatole France

> Everything will be okay in the end; if it's not okay, it's not yet the end. —Anonymous posting on a classroom door

In short, perspective is how things are viewed, the context in which we see them, as well as how we interpret what we see, how they appear in our own heads. In being able to foster change, embark on a long-term project, and achieve almost anything, perspective will play a key role and, sometimes, not a very helpful one.

Perspective is highly subjective, of course. Our view of ourselves and the world is cooked by our own learning and experiences, which become our prejudices and biases. In this cauldron, things can get pretty murky. "We do not see the world as it is," said Virginia Woolfe. "We see the world as we are!"

Because of this, perspective is at the same time the most critical element in learning and yet the most difficult element to teach. Essentially we are teaching change on an even deeper level than habit, although to be sure, ways of seeing become as routinized as any other habit.

It's tough, therefore, having ventured down any new path, to maintain the course, at least in part because frequently we are bringing the same old way of seeing things into this new paradigm, much like Springsteen pointed out in chapter 1. Our vision may have changed, our actions may have changed, our plans may have changed, but, of course, as Portia Nelson might ask, if we fall into the same old hole, are we going to see it, and ourselves, in the same old way?

Philip Roth once said that everybody had an idea for a novel, that every person getting onto the subway in the morning has an idea for a novel, but they just don't know where to begin (frequently, he noted, "I am one of them.") But while it may be true that beginnings are difficult, the ability to sustain the drive to write over a sufficient-enough period to actually write something seems at least as difficult, if not more difficult, than the actual beginning itself. As noted earlier, Malamud tells us the first draft is where it takes the guts, the ability to "live with the imperfect until you can make it better."

Students often imagine great writers and scientists and mathematicians, or really any successful person, as having been born great. They imagine great musicians, for instance, just picked up their first instrument and the sound flowed like honey—not so much as a single sour note. Most do not immediately see Edison laboring over the thousand seemingly unsuccessful experiments that preceded the invention of the light bulb. They rarely see the real process of creation as described by Samuel Beckett: "Ever tried. Ever failed. No matter. Try Again. Fail again. Fail better."

There are, of course, many reasons why this message gets disseminated and engenders in our students (and many others) the big Monday-morning winning X-Factor-supermodel-Master-Chef-lottery and getting-all-the-overdue-work-done-in-a-single-Sunday fantasy. Modern educators must now also counteract such extreme notions by being modelers of process as well by sharing the "drafts" of our problem-solving and learning acquisition. Teachers are usually not born understanding how to solve algebraic equations: the struggle of how the teacher got here, the means by which he or she developed the passion for the subject, is just as critical to learn as the subject itself.

Perspective then can be defined as, at least in part, being able to reflect on decisions, processes, and outcomes with some degree of objectivity while suspending any kind of "final" judgment. Admittedly this can be difficult to do, and something that we may not even completely be able to do, but nonetheless, it must be done to whatever degree it can be done in order to really find achievement.

This is a critical attitude because, as we all know, no path of change is without its difficulty, and no series of decisions will be without some less-thoughtful choices. What is clearly so important to teach is how to deal with these feelings that often overwhelm us: futility, frustration, self-recrimination, and their fellow travelers, which often keep us from being able to see things whole, in context, justly.

Reflection is as critical to finding success as is creating a vision and then acting with positive initiative in pursuit of that vision. Even as we move forward we must be able to reflect so that we can constantly adjust our bearing and, of course, even change course, when required, toward new visions.

Reflection is a critical component of perspective, but it alone is not enough. Our tendency to harsh self-judgment, though as common as weeds, is often the antithesis of successful success practices. A very talented painting student responded to an instructor's feedback by deriding not only her work but also her own nature. She wondered aloud if she was stupid for making the same mistake again, or merely untalented. The instructor asked why she was being so harsh toward herself.

"Because I have got to learn my lessons!" she replied.

"So," the instructor asked, "are you saying it's okay for me to call you talentless? Would you think it was okay for me to call you stupid? Do you think that would help you learn?"

The student replied that, of course, "it would make the situation worse."

"So, why on Earth would you want to be a crueler teacher to yourself that you would ever allow any other teacher to be to you?"

Reflection is critical, but it must be softened by a little kindness. As facilitative teachers we can exemplify (all of us can do with showing a little more kindness to ourselves and others) as well as promote this kind of perspective. One idea is to subject self-abuse (the verbal kind) to the same freedom-from-abuse standards you would expect from interpersonal behaviors. Many classrooms are festooned with signs warning of the consequences awaiting students who bully and abuse others. A family therapist suggests that it is not inappropriate, if you would give a child a time out for calling another child an idiot, to consider a similar consequence for a child calling himself or herself the same name.

Replacing harshness with a more positive view in self-reflection is one element of being able to measure progress in a way that continues to nurture progress. Just as harshness and self-recrimination are learned attitudes, so, too, can resilience and self-nurturing become learned. Having students revisit the creative problem-solving process shown in a previous struggle (even baby steps are steps) is a great way to reconnect to positive experience and begin to learn resilience. "We are continually faced with a series of great opportunities," according to Common Cause founder John W. Gardner, "brilliantly disguised as insoluble problems."

If we can learn to separate screwing up from being a screw-up, we can begin to take that distanced view of close things referred to earlier. Perseverating over what we have not accomplished, looking only at the distance yet to go rather than the distance we have traveled, does not have to be the life sentence of self-perception that impedes progress.

I was going to do some of my homework tonight, and the rest tomorrow, but when Simon, Theodore, and Alvin called me to go to a movie I couldn't say no! Now I'm never going to get it all done tomorrow. I'm such a screw-up, anyway, I might as well just hang out with those chipmunks again tonight.

This first element of building a meaningful ability to employ perspective is actually begun in the envisioning stage. Clearly vision that brings with it the possibility for long-term commitment is a driven by genuine desire. Others may well have had input into its articulation, but in reality those things done *only* to please others rarely evolve fully. To engage desire and passion strong enough to overcome lethargy, negative habits, and pessimism, the vision must be true and strong, and at least "somewhat" attainable, at least in the view of the person pursuing the dream. Jim Abbott may not have been able to knit but he was able to become a major league baseball pitcher, though many doubted such a dream could be achieved by a man with one arm.

To be sure, some decisions may have some "objective" value, and we would be poor parents and educators indeed were we not to try to intervene. Having several stiff drinks before setting out to drive a race car at 200 plus miles per hour is not a particularly good decision from anybody's perspective. Abdicating responsibility to guide and lead is far from good educational or parenting ethos: indeed the coaching model we are building here demands that we continue to facilitate planning until all the pros and cons have been laid on the table. However, we must also continue to reserve our own judgment, assuming there isn't any imminent danger, and bank on the fact that most people will choose reasonable and positive outcomes. More importantly the initial vision can, and probably will, ameliorate over time.

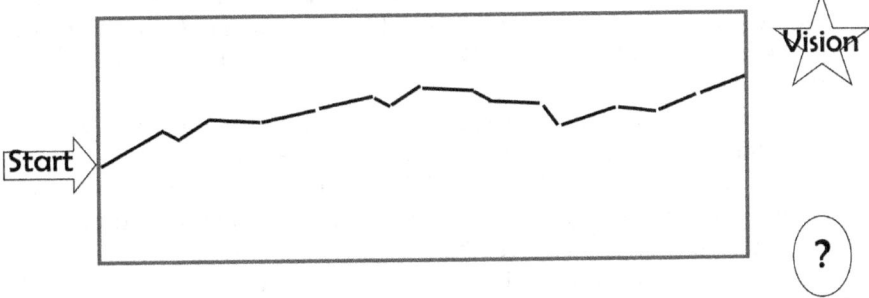

Figure 5.2.

Referring to figure 5.2, follow the line from the start toward the vision this person has set. Again as an example of a long-term process of progress toward a vision or goal, the line is hardly a perfect straight shot. The route is made of achievements and struggles, gains and losses, peaks, plateaus, and even precipitous falls. Persistence in the face of these doubts can be driven by a perspective that allows objective reflection without self-recrimination. "Striving for excellence motivates you," says psychologist and writer Harriet Braiker. "Striving for perfection is demoralizing."

A key element of perspective is embracing the understanding that the successful journey is often filled with imprecise steps. Dealing with a mess with dignity, humor, and hope, while you reflect and make adjustments, is also critical. Screwing up does not have to be a hugely painful experience; though, in all candor, the likelihood of removing its sting entirely is remote, if in fact it is desirable at all. Not wanting to feel badly is as good a motivator to do the right thing as is wanting to feel good. Properly facilitated, reflecting on and remembering how embarrassed you were when your teacher found that your brilliant essay was largely filched could be a strong incentive to do your own work in the future and not have to suffer the same feeling.

As we begin to act and break down the process into small goals, and succeed and struggle in our progress, vision also evolves. Sometimes the vision becomes stronger, more palpable, more possible. Initiative evolves into greater self-discipline and movement toward the goal. Reflection helps develop deeper faith in the probability of achievement, which in turn energizes us to "do what needs to be done." This is especially true when it comes to the critical ability to sublimate immediate pleasures for longer-term goals or to bounce back from a misstep or mistake.

Likewise, going off in different directions, rethinking the distant goal, being willing to slip down an interesting alley, all of these are valid as well, though they open us to more complex forms of reflection. "Not all who wander are lost," author J. R. R. Tolkein reminds us. Often in these instances, facilitative parents and teachers help students look at values and not just objectives. *There is a sneaky little voice in all of our brains that sometimes lies to us. He whispers, "Yes, you want this," when in fact you are just trying to avoid that!*

The ability to recognize the sometimes-subtle difference between being off track and being on a different track is a learned ability also, and critical to perspective. As Edward Albee wrote in his play *Zoo Story*, "Sometimes you have to go a great distance out of your way in order to come back a short distance correctly."

Perspective is also about being able to maintain balance. For example, looking at that balance between fun and entertainment, it almost goes without saying that anyone not suffering from anhedonia likes to have some fun. It's basically irrelevant whether fun is going to the movies or going to a rave. However, to maintain balance, you have to be able to reflect on that, too. It may well be pleasurable to go movies all of the time, or go to six twenty-four-hour raves per week, but is it feeding the goals you have set for yourself for long-term outcomes? If it is, great; it's fun! Fun means enjoyment in the "event" but also, on another level, engagement with the goal, thinking ahead, employing the opportunity to expand your work: fun is fully integrated into work and goals.

Sitting down and completing sixteen scenes of your screenplay is not of doubtful import, but you can also make some importance of raving if you are also consciously, meaningfully observing and filing away these observations for eventual screenplay use. However, when it is just the rave itself, for the purpose of the rave itself, that's entertainment. There is a time and place for each, and each has its place in a balanced life, but being successful is about keeping in perspective how to balance these desires. It is about setting up structures by which those sixteen scenes get written but so that the joys of life are not squeezed out in the process.

Ernest Hemingway, who apparently liked having a bit of fun boxing, fishing, hunting, killing, womanizing, and drinking (all worthy and estimable enjoyments to some), was also the self-same Hemingway who made sure that each and every day he wrote three hundred "well chosen" words before he allowed himself to leave his office to box and hunt and fish and drink. And if he wanted to take a day off, he had to write his way into a day off by producing an additional three hundred words for each day he wanted to slack off.

Perspective is also, perhaps even primarily, a means to measure progress and remain steadfast in the face of uncertainty. While it is doubtful that Hemmingway knew at the outset of any novel how many words it would take to complete the text, the sheer accruing of those well-chosen words signaled progress and measurable accomplishment. Counting worked for Papa as part of his "built-in, shock proof, sh*t detector" to help him find the truthful balance between work and fun and entertainment.

Additionally, withstanding the bumps and bruises one inherently encounters on the road to our greatest achievement is also a critical part of perspective. In an interview Joyce Carol Oates advertised her absolute certainty about her talent and how it allows her to sit down to write without a moment of self-doubt. Bully for her. For most of the rest of us, doubt plays a very powerful part in our perspective. Being attentive to this, planning and practicing how to deal with it, can go a long way to keeping one from drowning in the river of self-doubt.

Dr. Robert Brooks, author of *The Self-Esteem Teacher*, talks about this as instilling in our children "islands of competency," which they build up with their accomplishments as a means of building resilience. The more they accomplish, the more they build up their "island" and believe in their abilities to accomplish, the better they bounce back from missteps and setbacks, and the less likely they are to get washed away in a storm.

Some build their islands with the memory of accomplishment, some by laughing in the face of despair, some by finding some kind of rock that they can cling to: a person, a place, an idea. One teacher has been advising his students for years to pick some simple attitude-adjustment technique and just try to do it every day. Dance for fifteen minutes, go for a run, read a few pages of a joke book, whatever it takes. For him, his perspective is enhanced by trying to genuinely laugh at least once a day, and to always get a good night's sleep. Although he is not able to accomplish this every single day, he has grown to believe he can accomplish one or both often enough to be relatively certain that even on the darkest days, a better day is never far away.

We can teach resilience, courage, and perspective in our classes as well. For instance, Romeo and Juliet's tragedy is often taught with the idea that they are misunderstood and being used as pawns in the hateful machinations of their kinsmen. And they are, but more poignant, and even more tragic, is first Romeo's and then Juliet's inability to carry the burden of their sorrows with a bit of courage and hope.

A good question to ask is how might the ending of the play have changed if Romeo had the courage to live with the intensity of his emotional pain for even fifteen minutes after seeing Juliet seemingly dead? Clearly it would have been a different play. Juliet would have awakened, and they might have lived happily ever after. Or they would have had a desultory marriage that ended in an acrimonious divorce during which they savaged each other over who had the right to which magazine subscription and where, tragically, each used their own children as pawns in their hateful machination. However their lives turned out would have been, in all probability, less tragic than how their lives didn't turn out.

Perspective is yet one more thing. Perspective is not just about deep understanding, but it also about truly accepting that, try as we will, plan as we will, focus as we will, nothing is ever completely in our control. It is part of the realities, part of the challenges, but also part of the serendipity of the journey.

Referring back to figure 5.1, note that the ultimate destination at the top is designated by a star and the word *vision*. You'll note that the line of progress, in this example, has completed its trip a bit below the ultimate destination. At the bottom of the graph, however, below the word *vision*, is a question mark. The question, of course, is, Why does the star have the specific outcome of vision and everything else falls into mystery? It is a great question to pose to students when presenting this material.

Students especially, when showed this graph, almost always see the question mark as the opposite of whatever is defined as the vision. Say the student's vision is an A+ as a final grade in June; ask what the question mark is and they are likely to say an F. And it might be, but it might just as well be about 683 other things ranging from an incomplete to an A+ itself. In fact it is perfectly possible, you can tell students, to do not a single lick of work for the entire year, cut every single class, curse out the teacher, and still get that A+ as a final grade. After all, only so much is in our control: anything can happen, anything at all.

This idea was referred to earlier in mentioning how luck, such as the luck of being born to a well-connected family, for instance, can often mask enormous inefficiencies of thought and character. Such influences allow certain people the appearance and trappings of success, such as going to a top university like Yale, without actually having earned it. Hard to believe, but some people even get elected to important public offices based on such bamboozlement alone.

Want an A+ without doing any work? Here's how.

Pray.

That's it: pray for a computer glitch, or an earthquake that destroys all the records and swallows up the teacher so the administration is forced to allow the students to supply their grades on the honor system (an A+ in this case would assume one is not bothered by not employing honor). Or they could pray that at the exact moment their teacher is about to scribe an F as their final grade they are overcome by a brief paroxysm, such as a mild TIA, that short-circuits the teacher's brain. *Oh, yeah, that student was terrific this year, wasn't he? A+++++!*

Anything is possible.

The reality is that any series of decisions, no matter how well planned, how deeply thought out and measured, is subject to the whims of weather and time and circumstances, over which we have little, if any, control. A vision is most of all a guide, and initiator, perhaps even the main actor in the drama, but it is only one actor of a cast of thousands. This is what people who feel successful seem to understand that those who feel less successful may not. Yet, says Mark Twain, "It's the damnedest thing, but the harder I work, the luckier I get."

So if the opposite of a vision is simply an open question, perspective is as much about understanding what you can control as it is about understanding what you cannot control. At the end of the day, the reality is that nobody, not your mother or father, not your teachers, not even Oprah herself, can guarantee you a thing about the future, no matter how thoroughly you plan and execute your plan.

Critical skills, far from being a promise of absolute success, are more pointedly an instrument of limited power over what you chose to do as proactive or reactive decisions. However, while good decision-making may not keep at bay the stock market crash that wipes out your nest egg, it may well have caused you to have diversified enough to keep the pot boiling while you think of something else. What good perspective tells us is that if we stay committed to exercising good decision-making toward the fruition of our "dream," while we might not wind up exactly where we planned, at least we'll usually be in the neighborhood. Admittedly to some that is perhaps not enough; as they might say, *A house close to the beach is simply not a house on the beach, now is it?* For most of us, though, being near the beach is good enough, and maybe, like during a storm surge, even a little better.

One way to approach this idea with children and students is through a very simple equation: ask them to figure out how many days they actually go to school (a general accounting is okay). What you'll find is that, on average, most of us go to school for two thousand days (about sixteen years). Then account for the number of days that you will have to go to work over the next forty-five years or so. After you have racked up those numbers, you'll find your equation to be something akin to 2,000:11,000.

Think about this. Again, while there are no guarantees, most assessments equate more education to greater satisfaction, higher levels of pay, and often more contentment with life in general. Use this simple equation to ask a simple question: would you invest $2,000 to get back $11,000? If you could slack off for two thousand days of school to work harder for the next eleven thousand days, or if you could work harder for the two thousand and roll a bit easier from then on, which would you choose?

This is essentially the question almost always asked internally by successful decision-makers: What is the immediate impact of a decision in relationship to the longer-term impact of an outcome? Less academically and behaviorally successful students rarely do. To our discredit, although we ask students to do this all the time, we rarely teach them how.

This interchange between a dean and a high school student illuminates how we can sometimes thwart critical self-regulation skills while still expecting them. The student was a generally well-behaved, though fairly loquacious, young lady who had gotten tossed out of a class where the teacher's laminated, posted list of rules had as its first rule "Don't argue with the teacher." In the dean's office she was railing against the clear injustice she was being persecuted under.

"You were talking in class," the dean said angrily. "Short story."

"Okay, but it wasn't only me, and he never warned us or anything; he just went off and threw me out. It isn't fair."

"He doesn't have to warn you; he doesn't have to be fair. This is how it is. He's up there, and you're down here, and poo-poo runs downhill. Get used to it."

"You know," she announced to several other miscreants awaiting their fate, "if I ever even think even for a second that I want to be a teacher, somebody shoot me."

In fact, the dean presented this student with the most probable reality: that she had to accept and learn to live within the context of the limitations imposed by the teacher or pay the price for not complying. These unstated contracts are everywhere all throughout our lives: take the paycheck, plan on taking your vacation when your employer deems it appropriate. Don't like it? Don't take the job. Even had he said this better, the real shame was missing an opportunity to be a dynamic teacher and teach self-discipline instead of just being a disciplinarian.

Even though many relationships in school, as they are at work, are often defined by a clear hierarchy of authority, we still have the choice to be a certain way rather than feeling forced to be a certain way. This dean, had he been trained to help this student control herself rather than to merely control her, might just as easily have taken a moment to ask this student a simple question: What does she want out of this class in respect of grades, learning, and building a resume for college? Knowing what *she* wanted in the end might well have allowed her to go down the same path as desired by the teacher—that is, follow his instructions—but with a breath of fresh air rather than a mouthful of dirt. Teaching critical skills *is* about providing students with the ability to make empowered, *informed* decisions to make positive progress in their own lives.

However, in this instance what we do know is that this student left the interaction feeling disempowered, and enraged by the actions of the very people she was looking to for help. Once again we need to ask: Was this interaction intended in the best interest of the student, or for the dean, to make "managing" students easier? Compare the interaction with this student to the interaction outlined previously in chapter 3 between the assistant principal and that student regarding graduation. As a parent, even as a student yourself, which interaction would you find more desirable, and which is in the student's best interest?

Students need to accept realities, but they need to succeed in spite of them. Although the vast majority of teachers are not difficult, unyielding, and unfair, some are. It's a reality you cannot control, but you can control the process of how you will choose to deal with such a teacher. If you have guts, and grit, you will find a way to succeed. Applying self-regulation to manage interactions with teachers, employers, and others allows the student both to be compliant and to also feel powerful at the same time. This doesn't mean we need to abide abuse or not advocate in our own best interests.

Thoughtful self-interest can allow us to accept what we need to accept without impugning our self-esteem or rocking our foundations. In fact, the filmmaker Alexander Korda observed that the quickest path to any success is to "look like you are playing by their rules when in fact you are playing by your own." This is, again, a part of perspective, a part of how we choose.

Students acting in their best interests to gain something in the long term without feeling that they are swimming in "poo-poo" to do so is the essence of personal power. As represented in figure 5.1, it is simply that we can influence direction but cannot totally control it; we can control our decision but not the outcomes. But it does seem clear that the more we take control of our lives, the greater the number of opportunities we seem to have to bring a greater level of satisfaction into our lives.

You are a high school senior and figure 5.2 depicts your learning and growth through your high school years. You did fine: you could have done better but you chose, and rightly so, to also pack some enjoyment into your young years. No problem: you still did okay. Think of the scale now as a number in line that you have earned to pick your college. Now your number may put you behind something like 162,255 other students who worked just a little more diligently who will choose their college before you get to choose yours. Seems like a lot, but if you think not of the 162,255 people who may get to choose ahead of you but rather of the 7,864,992 waiting behind you to choose their college, you get a real sense of the impact of informed decision-making and self-regulation on your life. Imagining where you stand in line to choose what you do for work for eleven thousand days suddenly makes school effort just a bit more worthwhile.

This may not seem like a lot when every infomercial and self-help book in the world is trying to sell you some sort of pill guaranteed to make even your tiniest dream come true overnight. As teachers and parents we have to fight the world of fantasy but without puncturing dreams. It is a difficult dance, to be sure. However, getting control of one's life, making a purposeful connection between a decision made in the short term and a life you have imagined for yourself down the road, and having the perspective to recognize the accomplishment of progress, no matter how infinitesimal, is a mighty powerful pill indeed. And it works—double your money back guaranteed (certain restrictions apply!). One of those restrictions, however, is a very powerful one.

THE POWER OF NOW

Forever is composed of nows. —Emily Dickinson

The important thing is this: To be able at any moment to sacrifice what we are for what we could become. —Charles DuBois

The road of success is usually an arduous one, and vision, initiative, and perspective have a deeply mortal enemy that we must learn to vanquish, or at least tame. This enemy, this despoiler of dreams, this nemesis of change, this insidious creature who slips the guards and gets in behind our front lines, ruining our best plans with its enchanting nature, this all-time greatest killer of dreams, is the *power of now*.

Although little-known, leftover pieces of fried chicken, German chocolate cake, pizza, pastrami, and highly marbled dry-aged steak have secreted in them microscopic radios that broadcast subconscious signals. As the day wears on, as your once-powerful inner resolve begins to dissipate, as your strength and energy begin to wane, the radio signals get stronger and stronger, bringing you right to them, bringing them (as if they were an independent actor) right to your mouth seemingly of their own free will.

This is the *power of now*. Later, tomorrow, consequences be damned: *I want this now!* "Merciful heavens," cries out Banquo, fighting off the same temptation as Macbeth, "restrain in me the cursed thoughts that nature gives way to in repose."

Current brain research looking into the stop-and-go mechanism of the brain seems to validate what Shakespeare long knew and addressed through Banquo: *no* is a hell of a lot harder to employ than is *go!*

Reflecting on the concept of *now*, self-help writer Barbara Sher is not wrong when she notes, "Now is the operative word. Everything you put in your way is just a method of putting off the hour when you could actually be doing your dream. You don't need endless time and perfect conditions. Do it now. Do it today. Do it for twenty minutes and watch your heart start beating." Ultimately, Sher only sees the *power of now* as the protagonist in the story: a loyal assistant always ready to help carry a vision to initiative and beyond. However, vision, while not simple, is often the easiest part, and getting started, while more difficult, is still not often the hardest part. This perception assumes that once desire and will are in place, the rest is easy: *just do it!* You know that's all it takes! Long before brain-based research validated it, Mark Twain once observed that summoning up the will to quit smoking was the easiest thing in the world. "Last week alone," he said, "I quit at least a hundred times."

While not intending to oversimplify, assuming desire and will are in place, and one is trained to be able to see a short-term decision's impact on a long-term outcome, "just doing it" should be all that is needed. Make critical decisions that produce meaningful outcomes "and watch your heart start beating."

But all of this will, all of this resolve, all of this (assuming it is) genuine desire after a while, for most of us, seems to melt away, and become as toothpick-weak as a once-powerful steel girder on which acid has been eating and eating and eating away. When we only see the *power of now* as a protagonist, and not as the antagonist it can often be, almost all of our long-term projects will come crashing down.

Let's face it: the *power of now* is simply too powerful. Consider weighing the possible enjoyment of some immediate gratification versus the possibility of what you gain from immediate sacrifice and ask yourself just how long you will be able to deny yourself whatever it is that is looming before your eyes. Eventually, unless there is some kind of countervailing force, most of us will fail to reach our long-term goals. Self-sacrifice may be very tasty to some, but for the rest, martyrdom tastes a lot like eating cardboard and simply cannot stand up to a properly prepared order of *authentic* Buffalo chicken wings, with, of course, extra blue cheese.

So what keeps any of us from giving into the *power of now* all of the time? One key factor is teaching the truth about how we really use and apply our critical success skills. Resisting the *power of now* often enough is what makes any long-term outcome so difficult, but if we cannot learn to deal with it and the intensity of its power, we cannot move forward. Thoreau's admonition about morality provides good insight into how we can begin to tame the *power of now*. "Do not be too moral," he warns. "You may cheat yourself out of much life. Aim above morality. Be not simply good; be good for something."

The experiences of two remarkably similar men, let's call them Bill and Bob, really illustrate the concept. When each was young, each lived, more or less, moment to moment; neither planned in any substantive way about the future. They both enjoyed a lifestyle for many years that included much socializing in several bars, especially with women, and though both drank heavily, initially it was only occasionally to excess. Each was able to maintain regular employment, live decently, engage in athletics and cultural activities, and other than the drinking, live fairly healthfully. Though each was married, neither was able to sustain his marriage much beyond a couple of years, and neither has remarried. At a certain point, for each of them, the drinking started to get a bit heavier and out of control. At a certain point also each of them decided to try to get sober, and here the similarity ends.

Initially, when they chose to, both were able to stop drinking. Though he has experienced some dark and difficult moments, Bill has been able to maintain his sobriety for close to thirty years. However, Bob has wrestled with recovery a number of times over a slightly shorter time period. Although Bob has managed long periods of sobriety, as much as three to four years at a clip, he has also fallen off the wagon into some significant periods of heavy drinking. Worse still, each successive interlude has involved deeper depression and greater amounts of alcohol and only ends when he decides, instead of killing himself, that he will go back to rehab. As of this writing, Bob has returned to rehab again with the hope of regaining his sobriety.

One major difference between them is that while Bob has stayed in the same line of work, a somewhat lucrative though uninspiring fallback career, Bill used the intervening years to return to school and build a career in which he could be more satisfied and more creatively engaged. He has continued to evolve his interests, goes regularly to AA meetings, and while he has taken a less economically successful path than Bob, he has been able to maintain absolute sobriety. Though both have expressed a deep need to be sober, and an ongoing struggle maintaining sobriety (Bill noted in his thirty years of sobriety he cannot recall a single day when he did not want to drink), Bill succeeds every day, while Bob has only had periods (albeit long periods) of success.

Now again, without oversimplifying the complex emotional and medical issues involved here, it does seem fairly obvious that one reason Bill has maintained his sobriety has been that he has also made a concerted effort to rebuild his life. Bob has expressed the hope that by being sober he can build a better life and, while being sober definitely does enhance his day-to-day life, he continues to work at a job he finds increasingly physically challenging and intellectually unengaging. Typically, after a period of sobriety, when the "new life" Bob is hoping for does not find him, he grows more frustrated, more angry, and eventually, I suppose, finds an excuse to start drinking.

On the other hand, Bill has come to recognize, perhaps he has always recognized, that sobriety is a critical component of his being able to do work that he finds satisfying and pleasurable on a much deeper level than those pleasures that alcohol was able to provide. He is not just sober; he is sober for something, and hence he has been better able to counter the *power of now*, which in his case is that desire that is at least somewhere always in him, everyday, asking for a drink.

How we deal with decision-making in the short term, how we mine increments of progress for whatever joy can be gotten from them, is what makes this whole operation work. Absolutes about "goodness" and "badness" and "happiness" and "unhappiness" and even "successfulness" and "failure" as states of being rather than places we pass through as we move toward our visions in many ways make the *power of now* more potent.

Absolutes! That is teaching children and convincing ourselves, like in the Benny Goodman song, "It's gotta to be this or that." Absolutes weaken will because they create very fertile ground for slippage. The student behavior contract discussed earlier outlined an absolute. However, when victory or defeat hinges on a single mistake, you can pretty much guarantee failure. And once you have failed, you are a failure. What's the point of hanging on, what's the point of keeping on trying, what is the point of putting off what you are today to be a better something tomorrow if it all can go to hell in a heartbeat? To Oscar Wilde, "The only way to get rid of temptation is to give in to it."

Yet always giving in to temptation is just as bad as never allowing ourselves a break from being "too good." In the film *Hud*, the eponymously named womanizing, alcoholic main character gets a dose of reality from his aging father, whom Hud is certain holds a grudge against him for causing his brother's death in an alcohol-related accident. His father insists that was not their quarrel, and never was. "No boy," he says, "I was sick of you a long time before that."

"Well," replies a shocked Hud, "isn't life full of surprises. Well alright, I'll bite. What turned you sour on me, not that I give a damn!"

"Just that, Hud. You don't give a damn—that's the whole of it. You don't value nothin'; you don't respect nothin'; you keep no check on your appetites at all; you live just for yourself and that makes you not fit to live with."

Sacrifice is always a sacrifice, which we need to make clear: everybody wants their cake and to eat it without gaining weight, too. But when sacrifice locks its miserable jaws on us, its bite mark is a little less deep when we are sacrificing one thing for something better or for the realistic hope of something better. That is why it is so critical to spend the time helping our children identify their true visions and goals, whatever they are, rather than trying to get them to rally their excitement around goals that we have provided for them. In reality, the vast majority of goals and objectives that our students choose are the same ones that we would have chosen for them anyway, like college and meaningful careers.

However, a goal espoused by an individual is more likely to be embraced by that individual. Human beings quite naturally seek to protect what they helped create and tend to push off that which is forced on them. When our students or our children genuinely see the goal as their own, the ingredients for success are already embedded. A young athlete may not love to train but she will appreciate and enjoy the extra power acquired through training. A young student may not love giving up a raucous night of hijinks and revelry but will appreciate scoring a grade of which they can be proud.

While success in the long term is often the struggle to sublimate current desire for the achievement of deeper, more fulfilling outcomes further on up the road, that ultimate tradeoff, for most, cannot be fueled by belief that the further outcome will be worth the sacrifice alone. It is only the rare ascetic who can manage this level of self-abnegation.

Children, students, any of us understand the value of self-regulation when we really believe that such self-denial will result in something better, richer, stronger, nicer, tastier, down the road. But the *power of now* is powerful: it can overwhelm even the most stoic and committed. It is no accident that the greatest numbers of teen pregnancies are reported in states that require abstinence-only education, and limit both the knowledge and the availability of contraception.

The facilitative conversation here needs to help students determine what they need to keep the dream strong enough. Some need just to measure mistakes and to try to fix them, but others need the incremental supports, or vacations from the stress: the key is finding successes and building on them. Compensatory action arises out of our strengths, not out of our weaknesses. Our "weaknesses" are what are most prone to the *power of now*.

However, if we keep kids focused on those tiny increments, and train their perceptions to accept these inevitable fall-offs, messes, and mistakes as part of the learning that builds a better future, if they can allow themselves a break from being too good every once in a while, we can extend and accrue positive actions over a longer period of time. The *power of now* becomes much less potent when we learn that it is okay to give in, once in a while, so long as you don't give up or put yourself in harm's way. Somehow we have to learn how to make a pact with the *power of now*, to live in a world where there is temptation to which we can occasionally succumb rather than to live in a world of temptation in which we are always in up to our necks.

Frederick Douglass said that "without struggle, there is no progress." But the struggle can only happen when there is sufficient personal attachment and passion to the outcome to struggle, to want to excel. And it doesn't matter when the excelling happens: a taste for excellence anywhere creates the desire for excellence everywhere. Excellence does not happen in a vacuum, however. Paraphrasing Thoreau, if you want to be excellent, you must be excellent for something!

SIX

Exercises and Outcomes I

Skills

Who looks outside, dreams. Who looks inside, awakens. —Carl Jung

If you can find a path with no obstacles, it probably doesn't lead anywhere. —Frank Clark

OBJECTIVE: ALL STUDENTS WILL UNDERSTAND HOW TO OPERATE THEIR LEARNING MACHINERY

The intention of this book is to create a simple but effective way to teach students a set of skills that, mastered, has a pretty good chance of enhancing their ability to be successful in school and in life as well. However, learning a complex set of behavioral skills, rooted in a complex set of thinking skills, is, well, complex. It would be great to provide a recipe to follow, but even the simplicity of a recipe often assumes the knowledge of at least few complicated cooking techniques already mastered at your local neighborhood Cordon Bleu.

The reality is that success skills are learned and refined, relearned and re-refined all throughout our lives, so thinking they can be consumed and put to effective use in anything resembling a series of school learning periods is imaginative at best. However, what is possible is to put these skills into play, into thinking, into planning, into interaction, and into the life of the school. Some students may respond quickly, some may recognize its importance later, and still others may reject the ideas entirely. There is some evidence, however, that when these skills are taught consistently, infused in all classes and adult-student interaction, as it is done in *Tools of the Mind*, higher rates of success also follow.

However, we must be mindful that this program is not going to be "the fix." Even if there was such a thing, this would not be it. Programs like Critical Success Skills cannot compensate entirely for what is lacking in teaching, parenting, guidance, and administrative competence, or even for what may be psychophysiologically amiss.

That substandard teaching will produce substandard learning seems an incontrovertible truth. To divorce the need to be an intentional and effective teacher from facilitating students to develop success skills is also ludicrous. However, we have spent much of the early part of this decade (under NCLB laws particularly) believing that developing the delivery system alone will do the job of creating positive student attitudes toward learning and the results are equally ludicrous. The old adage, for instance, that behavior will fix itself if the teacher just teaches a better lesson has clearly been debunked.

Successful teachers and supportive administrators and much current research recognizes that positive, proactive behavioral strategies are as critical to building successful lessons as are clear objectives and active, engaging activities. Similarly, newer legislation has taken a more systems-oriented approach and seeks now to understand how each element of the system—governmental, familial, and professional—can be made more effective and in concert to produce better student achievement.

This intent is neither to blame teachers for the failings of their students nor to have students written off for the failings of their parents, but rather to begin a discussion of how we can develop the ability to help students develop the power to hold up their end of the structure. "Learning is not attained by chance," Abigail Adams said. "It must be sought for with ardor and attended to with diligence."

Although the practice of "content-related" teaching is addressed, except for some information in the next chapter, it is somewhat indirect. Facilitating the learning and practice of teaching critical success skills, however, is not meant to replace the need for teachers to think deeply about teaching, plan well for rigorous lessons, differentiate instruction, assess for learning, and engage students in interesting, outcome-aligned activities. Rather, it is meant to augment best-practice instruction with a facilitative, coaching-oriented approach that assures that students are able to analyze their learning practices and, in essence, *create a clear set of instructions as to how they can best operate their own learning machinery.*

None of us is born with a written operator's manual. Indeed, school, and life itself, is about writing and rewriting and rewriting yet again this operator's manual as each new version is released. Although there will be similarities, to be sure, an operator's manual for Steve 2.1 is going to be a lot different than the operator's manual for Steve 6.2.

This manual can but does not necessarily need to be written down. You will note that in this chapter, as well as many others, there are few illustrations, graphic organizers, and worksheets. This is by design. Although to be sure such learning aids are often useful, for the kind of reflective, inner-infused learning written about here, such exercises would be little more than busy work to make one feel as though he or she is making progress. Most professional educators are busy enough already.

While it is certainly useful to write things down, there is a truckload of difference between writing something down and being reflective about what you write down. It is also entirely possible to be reflective in a meaningful way without writing down one word. The objective is to help students and others create their individualized instructional manuals. Flexibility and thoughtful adaptability will go a lot further in helping students learn to self-manage much better than any invented "universally applicable" exercise.

One counselor in a New York City middle school had a student write down a detailed schedule for his evenings and weekends to facilitate his desire to complete all of his homework more consistently. And it worked! For another student all that same counselor had to do was get him to take a moment to review homework assignments he had already written in his notebook to achieve the same results. In both of these cases this counselor was doing exactly what needed to be done: facilitating student success by getting each to understand another line of instruction in the manual of their current and future success.

Lessons for developing and learning success skills, worksheets, and the like, if they are needed, ought to be created on an individualized basis. In reality, success skills are learned by trial and error, by thinking and reflecting, by trying new plans and, after assessing progress, trying a newly reformed plan again. For most, a vision of the future visits and we respond. Few ever write their life's plan out on a sheet of paper. Moreover, the reality is that if someone is disciplined enough to complete planning worksheets and to actually *do something meaningful with them*, they probably already have a foundation of success skills that they can build on. Busywork will not change lives. However, an ongoing, empathic, facilitative conversation focused on maintaining our children's and our students' engagement in planning, assessing, and measuring their own lives in compassionate and facilitative ways just might. Empowering our children to discover strengths to forge their own practices and paths in the end will largely work better than any paperwork. The real work of change is done not on scraps of paper but in the head and, more importantly, in the heart.

SIX PROFESSIONAL/PARENTING PRACTICES

> We need to remember, before we speak, that we are going to be the voices in our students' and our children's heads forever.
> —Karen Kanter

Success skills, as previously discussed, may be understood intellectually but are actually only learned through practice. Although there are some learning structures that have been effective in the past in teaching these skills, they are each, at best, just one more tool that will only work when properly used in the right situation. As the saying goes, a hammer is an excellent device for driving a nail but not quite so wonderful when applied to a screw. For the purposes of teaching critical success skills, every interaction is, of necessity, individualized and adapted for the needs of that person alone. Hence how we teach, and how we interact with students, becomes of consummate importance.

The *six professional (and parental) practices* outlined here create a foundational, active basis for effective success skill leadership. These practices are, essentially, a conveyance: a means to build effective communication and to help children/students identify and internalize the effective employment of the essential critical success skills: *persistence, self-regulation, workplace social skills, organization, time management, and decision-making.*

These six practices are (in no particular order of importance): *clarity, consistency, transparency, empathy/compassion, magnanimity (selflessness), and exemplifying.*

Now it is a shame that so many of the "practices" noted above have become dirty words in the annals of education. But just as Bono (from the band U2) announced during a concert, even though Charlie Manson insanely misinterpreted *Helter Skelter* as a call to wreak havoc and death, it was not the vision of the song. "Tonight," said Bono, "we take it back."

We, too, are taking back some misused and misinterpreted concepts and ideas. Properly interpreted and executed, they are critical not only to teaching how to achieve success, but also for twenty-first-century classroom needs as a whole. We are not just talking about technology, although that is an important component and one that we will look into as well. More importantly school, especially in how adults relate to students, is still largely a perfect rendition of the way teachers were instructed as youths and it is, unfortunately, largely perfect for another time. In the article "Schools and the Hidden Curriculum of Work," for instance, Jean Anyon defined many schools in New Jersey in the 1960s and 1970s, as, essentially, a feeder system for some fairly defined work expectations.

In one school in a wealthy community, a looser, student-centered environment gave the message that these children were expected to become decision-makers and follow their parents into corporate and political leadership. In another community where the expectation was that students would follow their parents into the local factories (when, of course, there were still local factories), a more rigid environment gave students the message that they were to follow orders.

These messages were given in complex ways, such as curriculum choices, and in seemingly simple ways as well. In the wealthy middle and high school, for example, when a student decided to go to the toilet, he or she merely signed out of the room. In the other school, where the expectation was that the student would someday be working on an assembly line, he or she needed to be granted permission by the teacher to leave.

While the economic shifts have altered school's vocational mission, the seismic social shifts of the last forty years have done little to change the relational paradigm. Many teachers still see their role as "middle-class" values mediaries: their role is to temper students into being dutiful and compliant citizens, and to help "place" them in society. This old relational order can be clearly seen in the usage conflict between the word *f**k* and the word *stupid*. The *F***ing Stupid Continuum* (the FSC) defines language that offends at one end and language that insults and hurts on the other. Essentially it defines the authority relationship in schools.

We'll go more deeply into the concept of vulnerability in the section about empathy, but to understand the impact of the FSC, we need to understand that school, for most students, is a place of great vulnerability. But of all of our vulnerabilities, none is more powerful than how our intelligence is perceived. Perhaps because school is that place where the constant judgment of intelligence and abilities is such a public act, our vulnerability in this venue ought to be more, instead of less, protected. That school needs to be made a "safe place" to learn is an oft-repeated belief among professional staff.

Yet the issue of language measured on the FSC reveals a different belief. For instance, in a school, really in most places, if you say the "F word" you are in trouble (we are *not* talking about using this word in regard to disrespecting authority, as in telling a teacher to go and f--- himself or herself). Merely dropping the "F bomb" to a fellow classmate in the hallway within earshot of a school official will engender what is laughably referred to as corrective action. Sometimes, for such off-handed remarks, punishments as harsh as suspension from school have been meted out.

Yet you can walk those same hallways from the first bell to the last machine-gunning the word *stupid* (or *retard* or any one of hundreds other degrading words in respect to people's race, intelligence, sexual preference, or even athletic abilities) and in all likelihood you will be able to maintain your demeaning tirade with little or no inconvenience. To be sure, many are offended by the F word (so much so that it even had to be euphemized for inclusion in this book) and this is not intended to advocate the free use of that word. However, the disparate reaction to each of those two words creates a stark contrast to this avowed desire to make school a "safe place to learn."

The late Sonny Bono said during a television interview that all of his life people had been calling him stupid. Teachers called him stupid, classmates called him stupid, writers in magazines had been calling him stupid, yet, he said, "I have been successful at everything I have ever tried. Song writing, music promotion, performing, running a restaurant and now even United States Congressman. So I really have got to take issue with that. I mean, Man, look at all I have accomplished! Seriously, how Goddamned stupid can I be?"

If Sonny is like most of us, he probably cannot recollect the numbers of times he had been offended by coarse or even insensitive language. However, here he was, in spite of all of his successes, with probably every instance of being called stupid, or made to feel stupid, seared in his memory. It is that way for just about everyone: probably you, too.

Educator John Holt believed that the primary reason children did not learn in schools was fear: fear of getting the wrong answers, fear of being ridiculed by the teacher and classmates, fear of not being good enough. Think about that in the context of the FSC.

Though schools are traditionally reluctant to change, the nature of authority in society as a whole has been utterly altered. For good or ill our current students do not offer teachers and school officials respect simply because of their positions. Of course, in case you hadn't noticed, few teachers offer administrators respect simply because they are administrators, nor can even President Obama expect to be respected simply because he is the president. In our schools, in our classrooms, in our society, leadership, as Dennis Sparks has written, "is no longer a position, it is an action. One can lead from anywhere."

Authority and respect, which used to be commanded, now must be earned. While *teachers must maintain authority* in their classrooms, the means by how that authority is established has become more complex and negotiable. Hence, the six practices outlined here can help create the means by which high expectations, such as building student responsibility for self-management, are negotiated, as well as how respect is given, trust is earned, and authority is held. Respect and trust are especially critical because the kind of change in perspective and behavior we are talking about ultimately takes deep, deep commitment. It is the kind of commitment that can only happen when the trust and respect are built over long periods of time.

Clarity and Consistency

At the end of the day *clarity and consistency* are really just two sides of the same coin and are ultimately about being "on message" and staying "on message" in a way that allows your child, or student, to habituate to (as opposed to merely being compliant with) certain kinds of positive, success-building actions. Too often character education in schools seems to devolve into some kind of lecture about what kids should do and shouldn't do. In other words, business as usual. What we are trying to do instead is move thinking and decision-making to the student, contextualized by their own genuine wants and desires.

Helping students practice and internalize the tools and skills they need, through facilitation and real-time, real-life application, is actually developing their capacity to build their own characters. In the end their characters, of course, just like the rest of us, and their lives are generally an aggregation of the decisions they make.

Clarity provides a means to understand what can sometimes be complex ideas: it is about finding simple ways of expressing ideas, without simplifying the ideas themselves. VIP is a perfect example. While thought and action can be very complex and difficult, through such a process of envisioning and acting on that vision in a cogent and meaningful way, the acronym does provide a simple reference point. Being conversant with the idea of VIP makes it easier to lock into these complex ideas with a simple entry point into a process that can, in fact, be accomplished by anybody, anywhere, and anytime assuming only the desire to succeed.

Clarity is speaking clearly, consistently, and powerfully. *Consistency* is also following through with integrity in all classrooms and, as much as possible, throughout the school community. These are both fostered through repetition of common language and even common references, such as using the story of the internal conflict of the two wolves as a way of having students address the internal struggle in us all. While constant repetition of thoughts, ideas, actions, stories, and examples may be exasperating to those of us who have heard them over and over and over again from parents, siblings, teachers, and elders, the fact is, we do remember them well and moreover usually wind up attaching some significance to them. Myths, as well as the repetition of phrases and stories, have worked very well indeed to deeply indoctrinate folks into all manner of religious and political ideology and action.

Everyone can recall phrases and statements and stories that they have heard over and over and can recall them wholly at the mere mention of a single word. The power of these remembrances, for good or ill, cannot be underestimated. How we develop delivery of this critical information and how we choose to facilitate internalization is exactly what clarity is. Consistency is agreeing to do this as regular practice in all classrooms, and as a community. Clarity and consistency will spell the difference between making learning critical success skills a meaningful platform for adapting to a changing society and engendering yet another bungled, empty initiative.

While admittedly developing common language in families is a simpler task than it is in school, where inputs are much more diverse and relationships are experienced over shorter periods of time, it can be done. It is especially important to build these communication structures among the professional staff in as facilitative a way as we would expect the staff to interact with the students. A school that chooses to alter the nature of its interactivity would need to also commit itself to developing the requisite acceptance of such a change, as well as to developing the interpersonal communication and listening skills also necessary to ensure significant impact.

Many teachers use the beginning of the school year as an opportunity to set rules and expectations for the year. The importance of this is exemplified by two seventh-grade teachers, an art teacher and a music teacher, who were both starting their careers at the same time quite a few years ago. The art teacher was frighteningly strict, but the music teacher was just plain sweet. All she wanted was for the students to love music as much as she did.

At first the students hated art class, where they felt imprisoned and fearful of even breathing wrong and *loved, loved, loved,* the music class where things were loose and *fun*! However, by the middle of the year, there was a huge change: the art teacher had loosened up and suddenly that class was fun. Music class had devolved, however: even the normally well-behaved students were being sent to the principal's office and everyone was out of control. When she wasn't throwing up her hands in despair, the music teacher was either screaming or calling for help. She did not return the next year, either. Rumor has it that she quit teaching to take a job as a guard in a maximum-security prison . . . for the stress relief.

Of course what had happened was that in art class the clarity and consistency of the teacher helped the students internalize limits. Her students learned exactly where the lines were that could not be crossed, and the consequences of crossing them. Because of that they were able to manage themselves, which left the teacher free to actually teach art.

It is unclear if the art teacher could get those same results with an autocratic approach today as she did then. However, while posting a list of rules, such as the one that had as rule number one *don't argue with the teacher*, may not work in today's classroom, the same effect can be accomplished in a more facilitative atmosphere.

Consider taking a couple of periods at the beginning of each year or semester to ask students to collaborate on developing a chart of *successful learning behaviors*. The fear many teachers often identify when embarking on such an enterprise is that if they allow students to create such a list, it will become merely a collection of goofs:

Rule 1: No homework, ever!
Rule 2: Class attendance is optional.

The key to avoiding disappearing down the nonsense rabbit hole is getting students to own some truth about their own successful learning experiences before opening the gate for the discussion and brainstorming. Get them to think about times when they actually learned, perhaps through a writing prompt, before beginning the process by which you create rules for their classroom. Ask students to visit a time when they really, really felt successful as learners. Such experiences need not have only happened in school nor even be school related. Learning, after all, can happen anywhere. Although for the most part you will get school-related learning victories, you may also be amazed at what proficiencies some of our most reluctant learners are achieving outside the walls of school.

You will hear stories of coaches and parents and bosses at work engaging our students in all kinds of amazing ways to help them connect their competencies to their accomplishments. Many students will discuss other classes, and talk about phenomenal experiences mastering complex subjects that will make your mouth drop open. But after all the anecdotes have been shared, drill down to what qualities were extant during these successes.

Doubtless you will have to wean them of such phrases as "I had a good teacher" or "It just kind of happened" to get them to be a bit more specific. Ask instead what qualities the teacher was exhibiting, or what qualities they were bringing to the learning experience. What you begin to evolve are classroom conditions under which students can be successful, and specific behaviors that often echo exactly those positive learning and teaching habits I've been writing about: teachers excited about their subjects, students paying attention, staying on task, everybody using positive language, being encouraging. Work at it a bit more and you can refine it into a series of behaviors that can be created into actionable items that both the teacher and student can employ to achieve learning success, such as:

- use encouragements instead of criticisms;
- listen more than you speak; and
- talk yourself through difficulties by reminding yourself that you have succeeded before.

Once you have asked students to base their suggestions for a great classroom on previous actual successful learning experiences, goofy gets replaced by an extraordinary list about what *they* must do, and *want* to do (and how teachers can help them) to foster a great classroom work ethic (you'd also be teaching cause and effect, by the way). The key behavior on the part of the teacher and the other students is to use the items on this list: in conversation, in application of behavior change, and as proactive activation to plan for and achieve successful outcomes.

A great example of this kind of proactive ethos-building was created, quite accidently, by a private-sector educational services company. Early on the organization started instituting a monthly "intellectual" development meeting. Its function was to keep the company always able to provide high-quality, cutting-edge professional development for a constantly evolving marketplace of educational needs. Consequently, trainers were hired not only for their abilities to provide high-quality training but also for their professional curiosity and their intellectual ability.

Initially, they were the victims of their own intelligence. Most of the development meetings would wind up becoming contests over whose wit and genius could rise above the others and, while these sessions were exciting at first, both enjoyable and stimulating, they were rarely productive and after a while even began to become a bit tedious. Recognizing this, they began to create and institute a series of "behaviors" that promoted maximum usage of time to focus on actual training development without removing the excitement of intellectual exchange. In all about forty behaviors were developed, each with a single, simple focus, such as:

- Do not allow personal obsessions to dominate the discussion.
- Listen carefully.
- It is everybody's responsibility to ensure that everyone is encouraged to contribute.

Before each session everyone received a copy of the list and reviewed the behaviors. Then everyone silently chose a single behavior to be attentive to that day, and the first activity began. What happens is that because you are reviewing the list of "productive" meeting norms to choose your one for the day, while you may be focused on the one, all the rest are fresh in your mind as well. You begin to self-regulate your behaviors over time, more and more, along with everybody else, and wind up infinitely more productive and satisfied with the time well spent in a fun way, rather than using the time only for "entertainment."

Imagine doing a similar exercise each day with such a list as you might have evolved in the previous exercise. All your students need to do before any school day, class, activity, or transition is quickly and silently review the posted list and choose just a single behavior to work on privately. It's a little like an affirmation, but it also teaches values of integrating habits of mind as well.

Transparency

Transparency is the willingness to be clear and consistent in a very public way. Transparency is the willingness to continue the discussion until all the questions that can be answered have been answered. Transparency is the willingness to explain. Allies are transparent. Teachers and parents that want to build solid relationships with their kids try to be transparent in all that they do when it comes to interacting with kids.

The concept of transparency has degenerated to an image of adults blathering about all the goofy things they did when they were the same age as their children, or still do even as adults. Transparency should not become an adult opportunity to unload, and neither does it mean you ought to reveal inappropriate personal information about yourself or others. It also, most explicitly, does not mean one has to be brutally honest (which is often brutal, but rarely honest). You are not transparent if you have the need to spill your guts about every personal issue, in every class, on every occasion. What you are is probably in need of a therapeutic examination.

However, transparency is particularly critical in the complex parent and/or teacher relationship, where authority is simply a part of the relational DNA. While clearly personal empowerment is critical to youngsters in order to take control of their lives and dreams, it is also critical for responsible adults to bear in mind the role of a thoughtful authoritative relationship in building the capacity for personal responsibility.

In that regard, transparency is simply the willingness to share what is now, what is coming, and what the requirements will be to get to that next place. Transparency is posting the classroom expectations and making sure that everyone has contributed and is buying in willingly. Transparency is creating clear rubrics for achievement written in actionable learning objectives and expressed in "student-friendly language." Most of all, transparency is exemplifying for students the "reasonable" self-reflection and thinking on which you base your own decision-making and helping students engage with their own progress in just that way.

Here is a great dismissal idea from a middle school classroom, the transparency of which is somewhat poorly executed. The teacher stood at the door and as each student exited the classroom from the previous period, she assessed each student's performance with one of the following statements:

"You did a really good job today."
"You did a so-so job."
"You did very poorly in class today."

In each instance the teacher delivered the evaluation without a great deal of "judgmental" inflection, and she intended to make the interchange helpful. However, since there was no specific information as to what each student did in class that day that was good, so-so, or poor, how effective was it?

Interchanges with children intended to promote rational self-examination and to eventually eliminate the need for constant external affirmation must be transparent and take evaluation out of a single person's hand. Although there is little doubt that building a reflective component into each class, or even each school day, can be cumbersome, like most things about learning, its complexity and the amount of time it takes to employ it does lessen over time with practice and increasing expectation.

The key is in not removing external judgment, which is powerful and important, but rather in adding internal self-reflection to the process. It is actually at the juncture of fair external assessment and clear, objectively driven self-assessment, both rooted in transparent, clear, and consistent expectations, that true self-regulation can begin. It is actually a fairly simple shift from the "me" (could be a teacher, parent, or whomever) telling the "you" how I think you did, to the me asking how you think you did today.

Blackstone Academy in Rhode Island put transparency at the center of their literacy initiatives and reaped huge reading growth as a result. Often struggling readers see reading as, virtually, a genetic gift: you either have the reading gene or you don't. But Blackstone demystified the process by which students learned to read.

They took several actions to create transparency. First they broke reading into identifiable processes and skills, and followed up by sharing and explaining the results of literacy assessments, which correlated outcomes to specific skills. Additionally, they made it clear through attitudes, modeling, and direct interaction that reading fluency was not an innate trait and discussed how specific learning in specific areas could have an impact on each student's ability to read. "If you want to get better at reading," the teachers said, "I think I could help."

Initially students had the same relationship with their reading grades as they did for any summative assessment: it was merely an identifier that gave one bragging rights or a good reason to stay out of the lunchroom. However, as teachers instructed and assessed students, they continued to track progress using the specific subset of reading skill criteria and helped students recognize progress. The more students saw the progress they were able to make, the more open they became about their scores and their struggles. Reading scores and levels of improvement actually became topics of conversation among students on their own.

The nature of transparency shown in Blackstone, empathic but honest discussions designed to empower trust and commitment, is actually being seen more and more as the key to personal and professional growth in many areas. Many businesses, including General Electric, one of the innovators of "stacked ranking," have dropped the opaque restrictions that limited the numbers of employees who could be high performers in favor of a transparent rating system that encourages all to excel without limitation. In schools, the evaluative models based on Charlotte Danielson's *Framework for Teaching* or the Classroom Strategies Scale makes self-reflection and objective oversight intertwined to produce meaningful, personal, professional growth.

In an interview in *The School Administrator*, Danielson notes: "When my framework was first published, a large urban district wanted to revise its evaluation system. It had been a terrible system—top down, punitive and arbitrary. They revised it based on my book and, you know what, it was top down and punitive! All they did was exchange one set of evaluative criteria with another. They did nothing to change the culture of teacher evaluation."

Later in the interview Danielson further elucidates that fostering successful personal and professional growth "involves professional learning and conversations with site administrators and teachers: the more conversation the better. Site administrators as instructional leaders must appreciate the role of school culture, a professional culture, a culture of professional inquiry. They must define teaching as not just what you do with your kids for six hours a day but also about building a professional culture in which everybody is still learning."

Just as the Danielson model helps create a transparent, interactive structure between teachers and supervisors, so too can creating a "rubric" of outstanding student behaviors foster open and meaningful dialogue in the classroom about excellent student performance (just as having rubrics defining expectations for teachers in respect of all of the traits mentioned in this chapter can go a long way in fostering cultural change). This becomes particularly compelling when, as suggested earlier, genuine student/teacher input is part of the process. This best-practices model encourages a high level of student performance without creating an overly critical atmosphere.

Just as teachers in a self-assessment model are much more willing to embrace professional responsibilities rather than to assume an inflexible, defensive posture, so, too, when students are a part of the creative process they are also more willing to see themselves clearly. Even more importantly the ability to be self-directed is increasingly becoming a critical component of the twenty-first-century workplace.

Teachers worrying that in such a structure all they will be doing in their workday is reviewing learning-behavior assessment criteria with students need only to ask how often they actually engage with administrators (and other supervisors) in the course of their own work. Teachers and parents that promote self-reflection, once we have acculturated participants to be comfortable within that structure, need only occasionally review student self-assessments. In much the same way teacher-evaluation models such as the Classroom Strategies Scale seek to make regular self-reflective teacher usage as focused, as accurate, and as meaningful as a thorough administrative review.

When such transparency is employed by teachers, students' ability to self-assess can be measured with as simple a procedure as a handshake or a word or two as the student exits the class. Instead of the teacher telling each student his or her evaluation, the question could be the student's to answer. Based on a rubric, for instance, a student could simply select an achievement level and offer a quick example of his or her behavior supporting the selection.

Transparency is solving the problem, together at first and then, eventually, the student independently, and how to get there over time. Transparency, rather than telling students what to think, or what they need to know, is about *helping students learn how to operate their learning machinery so they can think for themselves.* To be a really outstanding teacher, or parent, we must put a structure in place that plans for our obsolescence. Part of transparency, indeed integral to the teaching of all of these success skills, is the recognition that sooner or later, to paraphrase cartoonist Frank Clark, our kids have to learn to live well without us. The real success of parenting, though, is that after you have taught your child to live without you, when he or she no longer needs your input to make good decisions about life, he or she still has a warm place for you in his or her heart. The same can be said to be true of being a teacher.

Empathy/Compassion

Empathy and *compassion* are another pair of words that have gotten a dirty rap simply because, as I noted earlier in respect to the misinterpretation of Dr. Spock (the baby doctor, not the Vulcan, who is *Mr.* Spock), people misconstrue compassion and empathy as sympathy and even pity. They employ the concept as a willingness to excuse student behavior or to lavish praise on the most inconsequential of efforts. Indeed, as related to real empathy and genuine compassion, such misapplications could not be further from the true concept.

To a large extent the "self-esteem movement" (*misinterpreted!*) has been labeled as another engine of liberal American education failure and empathic teaching derided as little more than an endless barrage of huge accolades for little accomplishment. Misapplied, this supposed "advancement" has succeeded only in allowing American students to excel in inflating their self-estimation. "Failure is good for kids," one overly serious wag announced on a late-night panel show. "Kids need to be taken down a peg or two." At least George Carlin made a joke of it!

In fact, this particular example of headline-driven professional development missed, as do many of them, the fine print of the self-esteem movement. Being compassionate and empathic, much as was discussed around the idea of courageous compassion in chapter 3, is not showering kids with undeserved praise. Rather, it is a means by which parents and teachers can attempt to move the dialogue away from only what is wrong with kids to what is right with them also.

As I noted earlier really facilitative teachers appropriately praise kids for their progress not only for their (supposed) successes. But of course such praise must be contextualized in the larger picture of both the progress and the distance yet left to the destination. The empathic approach is to help somebody understand how far they have to go, but also how far they have progressed toward where they intend to go; not only what needs to be done but also what personal force they have already displayed that they can continue to exert to meet that next marker.

True compassion, or courageous compassion, is also, in large part (but not only) a willingness to hold your students and children accountable for the choices that they make. Often, this can create a great deal of discomfort in the parent or teacher assuring that the consequences are enforced. But that's where the guts come in. For any teacher or parent that cares, enforcing a serious consequence is a powerful and painful thing, and yet a worse message to give a child is that you can finagle your way out of the aggregate result of specific choices.

A particularly compelling story about this failure concerns a student whose troubles at home became troubles in school. His overworked single mother was inconsistent in his home discipline, and although he certainly had consequences in school—he was suspended several times—he was also charming and loquacious and frequently able to talk his way out of jams. Not surprisingly, eventually he started to get in trouble outside out of school as well.

His first arrest was for shoplifting, then petty larceny, minor assault charges (mostly fighting), and so forth. His age and contrition in front of the various judges got him out of those. Multiple convictions followed, including one for making threats, and another for drug possession. Each time, the sentences were suspended.

Many judges and public officials, knowing that incarceration generally leads to a lifetime of continued incarcerations, are understandably reluctant to put a kid into the "system." He insisted, however, that he "knew" he would always be able to get off. He insisted he "had the system down," and apparently he did, or rather he did until a judge finally sentenced him, a few years ago, to seven years for snatching an old woman's purse for drug money. There is no way of knowing, but it is an open question whether a serious effort to hold this young man to some consequences while continuing to develop his understanding and empathy to others might have resulted in a better outcome.

Clearly, though consequences are critical, they are effective only as learning experiences when they are able to be *experienced* as the direct consequences of personal decision-making, particularly measured against progress toward a personally defined goal. This is another aspect to courageous compassion: assuring that even in the most stressful times, the empathic conversation continues. Once a consequence is seen as arbitrary or capricious, or worse still as the result of some "grudge," it becomes punishment alone.

While this perception is frequently a matter of perspective, rather than objectifiable reality, the ability of a student to alter his or her perspective from one of victimization to one of self-empowerment is so important. Repeating an earlier-noted concept, many studies have shown that successful people often see the locus for control of their lives as emanating from within themselves. Less successful people often see life's fortunes as something that happens to them. How parents, teachers, and other adults wield their authority is often directly related to the child's ability to develop a sense of empowerment.

Building and sustaining student trust is difficult. However, creating an empathic, nonjudgmental relationship is the foundation to helping children imagine their way through the various outcomes of a possible choice they are planning to make, as well as in facilitating their reviewing the positive and negative outcomes of a decision already made.

Tools of the Mind has a neat way to teach developmental writing, planning, and self-management that is built on just such empathy. Before recess students "write down" a play plan. Depending on the age and the level of development, the writing may be very rudimentary or even idiographic, but such a device engages the students in writing development and at the same time creates a data record of their writing progress. Just as importantly, it asks students to make decisions, in advance, about how they want to spend their time.

What's important in reviewing these plans is not how accurately students have effected their play plans but rather how satisfactorily they have used their play time. If the outcome is to have physical exercise, whether a child has skipped rope or played kickball is irrelevant. Yet if a child has squandered his or her play time squabbling with other children, helping students review these plans and reflect on their outcomes in a nonjudgmental way is an important teaching opportunity. Empathy allows the young mind an opportunity to draw the cognitive parallel between the plans they prepared, the choices they made, and the outcomes that occurred. The more genuine the understanding, the more willing a student is to find and accept his or her responsibility, the more likely they are to apply new learning to the next situation.

Without the willingness to take the time to engage in the empathic conversation, such encounters rarely rise to the level of self-assessment. They become instead another string of words in the endless string of words that comprises the long teacher monologue that is often listened to but rarely heard. As the saying goes, nobody really cares about what you know until they know how much you care. More importantly, as Frank Clark has warned in yet another cartoon, "If you cannot find the time to help a child find the right way, somebody with more time will help them find the wrong way."

Dr. Robert Brooks has written extensively about the role of empathy in teaching. "People who are empathic have developed a mindset that asks, 'In anything I say or do, am I saying or doing it in a way in which other people will be most responsive to listening to me?'" Dr. Brooks observed. "In posing this question I am not suggesting that we assume the role of amateur psychologist, attempting to analyze every word we utter in every interaction we have (if we did, we are likely to become disorganized, overwhelmed, and paralyzed), but rather that we keep in mind that if we want others to appreciate what we are communicating, if we want others to respond to and work cooperatively with us, then we must consider their perspective and how they perceive us."

The more students can internalize through our interactions that they have some power in their lives to create positive outcomes, the more they will be able to take on the responsibility of decisions that will produce these outcomes. "Optimism," says educator Nicholas Murray Butler, "is essential to achievement and it is also the foundation of courage and true progress."

However, believing you can only works if, after a while, you *actually* can. And when you actually can, and when you can see that "can" as having emanated from your personal action, you have started to build that belief system, those *islands of competency* we referred to earlier. Empathic teachers and parents help children identify the evidence of "can." Sometimes it's small, sometimes major: size doesn't matter, but sight does! Sometimes success is hard to see.

Think of house painting as a metaphor. Anyone who has ever painted a room a starkly different color can easily build a belief in their eventual success from the progress evident from even the first brush stroke. However, assessing the success of a second coat is another matter. Progress is sometimes easy to assess, and sometimes more difficult. Empathic response allows us to hold the light (for ourselves and to help others) from a different angle to see how you have progressed where seeing progress may be as difficult as seeing the slight color variation of a second coat of the same color.

Empathic, facilitative teaching is based on these interactions that allow students the opportunity to develop less self-judgmental reflection through which they can not only see but also *value* those incremental successes, especially when they are hard to see. In effect, rather than merely informing students of their progress, we are helping them hold the light at different angles so they can see their progress for themselves. While in structured teaching the *way* students learn is sometimes more important than the *what* students learn, in teaching critical thinking and critical success skills (as we will see when we look at planning a little later), the way is always more important.

Learning to manage the evanescent process of learning, through empathic understanding, is a key success behavior and a huge part of learning to operate one's learning machinery. Managing the process is always reminding yourself that you can, and validating this perspective with an empathic assessment of progress and previous success. Initially driven by external inputs that are consonant with internal beliefs, success becomes real and meaningful. Each success, *recognized and believed*, builds up the height and strength of Dr. Brooks's *Islands of Competency*. The bigger and stronger they become, the less likely our islands will be washed away by one or more of life's many storms.

Magnanimity/Selflessness

As Malcolm Gladwell reported in *Blink*, students can read a teacher's nature and potential effectiveness rather quickly and surprisingly accurately. This makes sense: regardless of the class, grade level, or curricular focus, the one subject every child has learned most deeply has probably been teaching.

Ask a young student to mime almost any profession and you will see all manner of interpretation; ask a young student to imitate a teacher and the vast majority of them will stand in front of the class, eye bearing down on the other students with a scowl on his or her face and a lofted finger shaking in rhythmic disapproval. Assign an older student to create a lesson as a learning project and they all stand in front of the room, lecturing. Students observe and study hours and hours of teaching every day and become experts in what teachers actually do.

Because kids understand teachers so well, ironically it is *not* the less caring teachers or incompetent teachers that are the most destructive. Most students read them out right away, not that they don't appreciate the respite they get from a hectic day by sitting in a classroom with little or no requirements. A careless teacher, the ones who mostly plan poorly or not at all, or yammer in the front of the class pretending he or she is actually teaching something or who provide a clubhouse, may well get away with it administratively from recruitment to retirement, but students know they are useless, and while they can enjoy them for the benefits they supply, they are little respected and marginalized.

Worse are nasty teachers, dyspeptic souls whose hatred of themselves and their own incompetence has formed itself into an inoperable bitterness and negativity. While worse, they are still somewhat able to be marginalized. At the end of the day many, but unfortunately not all, students are able to separate out the teacher's self-hatred from a personal estimation of themselves.

While it is true that there is significant accrued lost time and lost progress, many students can weather such semesters and emerge able to recoup the gains they might have had during a better learning experience. This is not to say this is acceptable damage: it is not, and never will be. Donald Clifton, the pioneer in strength-based psychology, noted that it is our responsibility to "make sure there is a teacher in every classroom and a leader in every school who cares that every student, every day, learns and grows and feels like a real human being." To be sure, most teachers either do, or try to do, this.

The real damage, I think, and so what defines why *magnanimity/selflessness* is a key behavior, derives from the need of some teachers (and leaders and parents, too!) to put their own needs constantly before the needs of the children. Now, of course, lines are crossed from time to time, and of course it is very important to maintain a balance between serving others and serving oneself. However, the ability to be *magnanimous,* and effect even a modicum of *selflessness,* is critical to the facilitative relationship and part of the means by which students get to develop their own strengths and success skills.

Wilber Dungy, a teacher and the father of football coach Tony, said, "The sign of a great teacher is someone who brings out the best in every one of his students, someone who can do it without tricking them, or bullying them or wanting credit for their achievements."

To be clear, when we talk about putting personal needs before those of students or children, I am not writing about this in the ultra-extreme. Such horrifying sociopathic manipulations as those perpetrated by Jerry Sandusky and Pamela Smart may well represent the failure of selflessness on a mind-boggling scale, but it is, thankfully, somewhat rare.

An incident of intended levity by teacher Gregory Sullivan, when he left his Merchant Marine Academy students to watch a film by themselves shortly after the Aurora shootings, is a more clear, though still somewhat extreme, example. As Sullivan left the classroom he warned his students that if "anyone with orange hair shows up, run for the exits." The resulting media flapdoodle over the highly apologetic Sullivan's firing (which ultimately morphed into only a temporary suspension) seemed to concern itself mostly with supposed free-speech incursions. A storm of *Foxtalk* railed against how such a bleeding-heart, politically correct, overly sensitive overreaction to a teacher's offhand joke, made without the knowledge that one of his students was the son of one of the victims murdered in Aurora, was robbing the teacher of his rights.

However, the real issue is not that Sullivan made a mistake or a bad joke; those are, for the most part, forgivable errors of judgment. The real issue was Sullivan's failure to put forth even a small degree of selflessness. Had he taken even a single minute of his free time to review work- or student-related emails, he would surely have noticed a urgent request from the academy's director that all staff be especially attentive to this young man in light of his recent horrific loss.

More commonly we see the result of this failure in relatively benign ways that all of us are guilty of from time to time. Who hasn't at one time or another chosen a TV program or a ball game instead of reviewing student essays that have been sitting on your desk for days? Who hasn't at least a few times spent insufficient time planning because something else more compelling came up at the last minute? Who has not said something in frustration or anger that they later regretted? In the scheme of good teaching practice these are often small matters that can sometimes be repaired with a genuine apology or a renewed commitment to professionalism.

However, the most problematic element of this failure to put the needs of the students before your own needs does sometimes result in great difficulties, but never more so than when the teacher (or parent) himself or herself is absolutely convinced that their self-serving mission is actually in the best interest of the kids.

As said a zillion times already in this book, human beings (including Mother Theresa, really!) are driven in some way, shape, or form by self-needs: the desire for wealth, or for love, or for self-definition as it is reflected back to them in their own eyes or the eyes of others. We are a complex bunch, we human beings, are we not? It doesn't take a whole lot of research to find examples of how the needs of others become subsumed by personal need. They range from the rather benign "I'll call you" lie to the somewhat-more-distressing "I swear on the heads of my children this mortgage-backed security is a 'can't miss' investment!"

More rare is finding someone who went out of his or her way for you, stood up for you, made a point of doing a kindness. Journalist H. L. Menken observed that reviewers sometimes overly harshly panned what they were reviewing. A negative review, he understood, promoted the reviewer, but a positive review promoted the play. A simple test to assess your own level of consideration is to try to compare how many times you have registered a complaint when things were not right in a store or restaurant as compared to the number of times you took the same amount of time to register a compliment for exceptional service or consideration.

It may well be true that that the survival instinct deep in humans causes them to see their responsibility as being very limited to others. However, it does also seem right that those who become parents (by choice or accident—it makes no difference), or enter a service profession like teaching (by choice or accident—it makes no difference), also develop *some* selflessness and learn how to engage with those under their care in a way that limits personal need without, of course, completely abnegating oneself. This is particularly true in the latter, professional choice: nobody made you be a teacher, and nobody is making you stay a teacher.

This is a critical change that has to occur, at least somewhat, for the common language and common practices of teaching critical success skills to evolve. The culture in schools too often still favors teacher needs over student needs. A guidance counselor, admirably recognizing that her waning empathy for the struggles of her students was limiting her effectiveness, recently chose to retire instead of hanging on for a few more years. Yet she was still very forgiving of her several "burned out" colleagues not in a financial position to do the same. "You can't expect them, after fifteen or twenty years, to give up their security and pay levels to go looking for new work," she said, "just because they find themselves tired of their jobs."

Neither do we want to create helplessness by letting the pendulum swing too far in the other direction so that every student sneeze is met with an adult holding a tissue. The point of balance is found creating a focus on building relationships that foster the capacity for student independence. In much the same way that we write objectives for specific learning, we must also have clear objectives in facilitation so that when we assist a student, the end point is not just a fixed problem, but a student who has learned how to fix his or her own problems.

Another component of selflessness is also to be clear that when we make a decision regarding students, we ought to be able to identify, exactly, in whose interest this decision is being made. For instance, do uniform testing protocols, such as those that limit the length of time students get to take a test, genuinely give us a fair assessment of each student's learning, or are they in place to make the administration of such exams efficient? This does not mean it ought not to be done. Sometimes management decisions must be made in the best interests of the organization, which at some juncture translates into the best needs of its individuals. But in our planning, discussion, and execution, we must strive for clarity where and when and how the needs of our students are being met to be as accurate as we can that the needs of our students are not being subsumed by the needs of the adults, or the organization.

We have already discussed exchanging judgment for facilitation, particularly when keeping one's personal estimations of a student's potential out of the conversation. Does a ninth-grader really need to hear that they have no potential as a scientist, or writer, or even as a college student, or is it only the teacher who really needs to say it? Indeed, many people who have gone on to success in all manner of careers have spoken of experiences where they had been told they had no potential for such a career.

One young man, just a few years ago, made his first mission after graduating to bring his medical diploma to his third-grade teacher. She had responded to his desire to be a doctor by informing the rest of the class that, since he was retarded, he would be able to do no such thing. Compare this to a different young man who, after being shunted to a vocational program, was encouraged to believe he was more intelligent than he was being given credit for by his welding teacher. About to receive his PhD, he just recently became the principal of a school and could not wait to share this news with that teacher. As a parent, which experience would you prefer for your child, and even more importantly, which teacher would you prefer to be remembered?

When teachers are unforgiving, whom does it serve? Put this in any other context and the answer is clear: forgiveness allows a relationship to continue unimpeded; not forgiving essentially limits or ends the relationship. However, if part of the process of learning an *academic* subject is periods of not learning, is it not equally applicable to apply the same process to learning personal behaviors? One teacher, at a staff meeting, declared she gave every student who messed up a second chance but that was it. "Nobody gets a third chance," she said. "I won't be taken for a fool!"

Another teacher announced during a professional development session on the importance of proactive classroom management that he would be more than happy to offer a student praise if one of them ever did anything worthy of praise.

An assistant superintendent at a large (and failing) urban district might believe she disagreed with such a sentiment because she publicly stated she believed in giving students "every opportunity to fail." The only problem was, of course, she didn't understand the nuanced difference between her statement and the idea of giving every student a chance to succeed!

These are not semantic arguments. These statements reveal a deep set of negative values toward students. To unmask them as the failure sentences they become, extrapolate such a remark into academics: *I taught Timmy addition, and he didn't get it, so I taught him addition a second time. But when he refused to understand it the second time, that was it for me. I will never teach Timmy addition again. I will not be taken for a fool!*

You'd be hard pressed to find a school district that would hire someone with an attitude toward academics such as the one outlined above, yet in many quarters such attitudes toward behaviors are not only extolled but also encouraged.

Anyone who has succeeded in staying married or maintained any kind of relationship over a period of time must absolutely be conversant with the ability to be forgiving, and sometimes forgiving in a selfless way. Understandably this is kind of generosity is made more difficult by the fact that teachers must learn to have this level of understanding and care with kids who may well have natures that are difficult for them to tolerate. However, being empathic is a critical teaching attribute, at least as far as teaching critical success skills is concerned, and the role of selflessness is embedded deeply in the ability to be both empathic and forgiving.

There are plenty of jobs out there where you can be as harsh as you want to be and get paid for it, like being a TV judge. Based on the huge ratings, viewers must get an enormous vicarious jolt from syndicated small claims judges. Their quickness to abuse their authority to demean and harshly characterize people brings peals of laughter from their audiences. People are often characterized as ignorant, and referred to as *stupid* or as *idiots*, and it's made clear that they are the intellectual inferior of these judge personalities. In one judge's case, her treatment of a defendant, who appeared before her in a case concerning his son, was so cruel, demeaning, and humiliating to the adult that it tipped over into sadistic and left the child bawling as a result of having to witness his father's humiliation.

However, does a judge have to be *harsh* in order to pass *judgment*? There are many judges whose unfailing courtesy and respect of those before their bench in no way diminishes their capacity for the sound and fair disposition of a case. However, the entertainment value of their court might not propel them to stardom and a multimillion-dollar income. Paraphrasing Menken, you might concur that judicial restraint highlights the importance of the law; judicial excess highlights the importance of the judge. Likewise, a measure of selflessness in teachers highlights the importance of the student and of learning.

An incident that clearly illuminates an example of selflessness occurred in a dispute between a journalism teacher and a chairperson from another department who was not his supervisor. A situation emerged in respect of an article one of the student journalists was writing about a number of teachers who had recently left the school. One of the teachers who resigned actually did so in advance of nonrenewal (a very common practice in schools), but during an interview his department head bragged that in fact the teacher hadn't resigned; she had fired him!

Later, reconsidering her remark, she called the student into her office and decided to fix her mistake by first asking, and when he refused, demanding to see the article he had written, saying, "I am an administrator and have a right to see what you're writing about."

In fact, the student journalists were encouraged to read back quotes during an interview to assure accuracy and build positive relationships with "sources." However, they were also taught that their notes were as private as they chose to make them. Just as professionals were, reporters were answerable to their editors and to their readers for fairness, accuracy, and objectivity. However, because of the unique place of student journalism, the journalism teacher did have final article approval before publication.

The student readily offered to read back his quotes, but it was not accuracy that was the problem. When the young reporter refused to comply, she threatened that he could forget ever getting a letter of recommendation from her, or from anyone in her department. She also said that she would refer the matter to the principal as student insubordination, a crime punishable in that school by death before a firing squad (however, because it was a school-related activity, the condemned would *not* be allowed a last cigarette).

Upset, he offered to show the journalism teacher his notes to attest to his accuracy, which he was told he did not have to do, but he was asked if he was sure he had gotten it right. "I repeated it to her," he said. "I asked, 'You really fired him,' and she said, 'You bet.'"

However true that she did not recommend rehiring, the reality was that once this teacher chose to resign, as far as the public record was concerned, his resignation was the only reason he left. In other words, this supervisor made a public statement in clear violation of this teacher's rights. Because in most schools the Board of Education is essentially deemed the publisher, such a quote in a school newspaper conflicting with public record could result in legal action brought by the teacher if he so chose.

To empower this student to think through the rewards and consequences of his actions, and to decide how he wanted to go forward, instead of just fixing the situation, the teacher discussed how the complaining chairperson certainly had the right to, or not to, recommend him for anything and was free to influence (though not demand) others to feel similarly. She could not, however, grade him more harshly than someone else as a punitive measure, nor claim he violated some school rule if in fact he had not.

He insisted these were not his concerns: he was willing to accept her consequences because he was certain he'd gotten the story right. But then the teacher asked if, in the case that something he wrote might be damaging to someone inadvertently, would the student be open to revisions. Without hesitation he said, "Of course," and then, when the situation was explained to him, he willingly removed the quote. "Why didn't she just tell me that?" he wondered.

Rather than asking for help, the chairperson continued her tirade on several fronts. Claiming her supervisory "right of review," she confronted the journalism teacher, and when rebuffed, made vague threats. "Students come and go," she said, "but colleagues will be here year and after year. I think you better think about that!" Finally she took the issue to the principal and superintendent, to no avail, and back to the advisor several more times.

To be fair, she also never followed through on her threats toward the student. He remained in her class and suffered no ill will. However, the shocking lack of willingness to get outside of her own needs to serve the learning needs of students, to even humanize herself or admit to a mistake, was made chillingly clear by how little she actually valued the students. In the end, what could have been accomplished with a simple request to a student's well-meaning nature devolved into (albeit fruitless) threats and intimidation that is really the antithesis of the kind of teaching relationship we are trying to create.

How powerful will our teaching and leadership become when we can achieve the ability to give of ourselves without losing ourselves; how powerful will we be when we use our own vulnerabilities to show how deeply we care and to teach what caring really is?

Exemplifying

In Stephen Sondheim's brilliant lyrics for his musical *Into the Woods* are these words: "Learn. Children may not obey, but children will listen." Children will see, children will listen, and they will learn. Do not be mistaken: *Students learn their teachers better than they learn the lessons they teach.*

Exemplifying is the final, but, in some ways, the most critical component of the core teacher/parent behaviors. In pondering the application of behaviors meant to induce students to understand, practice, internalize, and employ critical success skills, being a good example of the very things you espouse is of consummate importance.

While the "do as I say, not as I do" mentality that defines many adult/child relationships has some validity, as a specific teaching measure it is often wanting. Modeling procedures, attitudes, values, and skills is a critical part of the acquisition process for the nascent learner.

While many respectable professionals might disagree that they must be examples, I ask you to consider if there really is no relationship between the way students will embrace being accountable to deadlines and the way the teacher goes about his or her business of planning, collecting, and returning student work. How convincing is a teacher's trying to express the value of attendance who seems to get sick only on Monday and Friday?

To be sure, a great many teachers, if not the vast majority of teachers, are incredibly dedicated. Not only do they take few days off, but they also freely donate their time by working late, spending countless hours carefully crafting lessons and preparing, using much free time to communicate with students and their support networks, and coming in extra days to support student activities. However, below are actual comments by teachers that have been recorded as well:

"I think it's alright for me to slip out of school to go golfing. It is really for the kids more than it is for me! I come back so much more focused and ready to teach."

"I would leave a lesson plan but, what's the point! Subs never do the lessons anyway."

"Hey, they're my sick days. I have a contractual right to them!"

Just for the record, sick days are contractually defined as days that are to be used when you are too ill to come to work; personal days are for anything else, and, legally anyway, feeling badly about yourself or your job does not constitute illness.

The real damage, though, is in the area of respect. Behind the facade of students' happiness engendered by having a sub in the classroom, frequently there is genuine disdain. More importantly, the underlying disrespect makes any effort at promoting values-driven decision-making suspect. In one school students identified one teacher as having exemplary courage because, though he had a ton of sick days in the bank, he returned to school on crutches the first day he was able to after an operation for a necrotic bone. He was told to take at least a month but felt that since he was actually able to manage, it was the right thing to do for his students.

Mario Cuomo recognized this. "I talk and talk and talk," he said, "and I haven't taught people in 50 years what my father taught by example in one week."

Exemplifying the essential values you are trying to teach, whether it is about success skills or metacognition or interpersonal values or even guts, requires neither parent nor teacher perfection. *Exemplifying* requires only that you try, as best you can, to engage with those successful and appropriate behaviors you're promoting or, if you are not quite where you need to be in respect to living those values, that you are willing to share the process by which you are learning and internalizing them.

For instance, if your desire is to have your students interact with you and with each other in a more respectful way, you might consider refraining from discussing the "abject idiocy" of a colleague in front of the class. You might even consider adopting a pleasantly professional tone for your public interactions with them as you pass in the hall. Behaving in a professionally reasonable way, being able to function in the social environment of work, is powerful.

One study notes that it is not the ability to learn the mechanical and mental functions of work that costs most youngsters their first jobs. More than anything else it is because they do not know how to keep their professional lives from being driven by their personal feelings. The poet Robert Frost deemed education as the ability "to listen to anybody without losing your temper or your self-confidence."

You are not required to love your enemies, at home or at work, but particularly in school you are required to always be aware that through your interpersonal actions with students and with your colleagues, you are always teaching how best to handle the relational stressors that are always central to any position where humans interact with each other. It cannot be said enough: students learn their teachers better than they learn the lessons that they teach! In short, your bile has no place in the public sphere. That's what teachers' lounges were invented for!

One of the reasons for primal reactions in relationships, and in expressing personal emotions, is that many lack the linguistic nuances of examining and expressing their emotions. Anger is always fury because it was first learned at the extreme. However, this is one problem that can be solved through education. Many teachers have answered the call by creating "emotional" word walls that both the teacher and the children can use to express the nuances of their feelings. If someone can learn to define their anger along a continuum from enraged on one end, to slightly miffed on the other, they likewise can define and manage a more appropriate response more in line with the nuanced feeling.

"If kids do not have the skills to understand what they are feeling and how to properly label it, and how to regulate their strong feelings when necessary," said Dr. Maurice Elias, a leader in the social-emotion learning field, said during a recent interview, "they will not be successful in the classroom."

Take, for instance, a young child who, though he appeared to be fairly happy, suddenly declared one day that he wanted to "kill himself." Understandably alarmed, the teacher informed administration and his parents. A professional determined that the declaration was more a measure of frustration than actual ideation. However, to be proactive the parents and the teacher, instead of dismissing the child's feeling, began to question it on an expressive level.

"Do you mean you want to hurt yourself, or are you just expressing being upset?"

"Upset."

What kind of upset? Are you hurt, angry, frustrated?"

"Frustrated."

Frustration, as opposed to a more extreme expression, often has a specificity that reveals a fixable component or at least a more manageable level of emotion. Focused questions can quickly reveal a solution the child himself can apply and, as in this particular case, each learned nuance eliminated the need for the more extreme response. As the child learned more varied expressions of his feelings, the need for overwrought exclamations declined and eventually disappeared entirely.

Politeness, kindness, and courtesy in the classroom should be exemplified by the teacher so that it can expected of students. The no-bullying zone applies to the staff as well as the kids. One teacher from a parochial school, requiring an essay of a particular length, thought very highly of the fact that she papered the doorway with a student's (admittedly somewhat modest) writing submission that had the requisite number of pages but with huge spacing and exceptionally wide margins. She took great store in the fact that his humiliation engendered a more serious revision. Bully for her, literally.

It was no better when an assistant superintendent in a full high school auditorium called out a student in the audience for quietly chatting with his neighbor while she read from her carefully prepared lecture given to meet the district's antibullying education requirements. She stopped midsentence and demand the student rise and share what was so important that he had to speak while she was speaking.

"Nothing," he replied. "It was nothing. Sorry."

She insisted he rise and speak, but the student, clearly embarrassed already, demurred. When the assistant superintendent redoubled her efforts to force the student to humiliate himself, another student rose instead and sarcastically challenged the speaker. "Isn't this an example of the bullying that we're not supposed to do?"

As an educational leader, she certainly must have taken great pride in the fact that these students understood the message she was trying to promote.

Take any ideal from lifelong learning to persistence to organization to time management and there is a pretty good chance that if parents and teachers are not exemplifying it, the kids are not learning it either. It's really quite simple. If you want students to learn how to accept responsibility, simply do so yourself! If you screw up, *apologize*, and make a sincere effort to do better. Screw up in public, *apologize in public*, and make a sincere effort to do better. Honestly, that's all there is to it. At the end of the day, our children look to us not for perfection. Rather, what they need from us is something tangible on the higher scale of positive human behavior that gives them the ability within themselves, as Abraham Lincoln said, to seek their "better angels."

A great example of exemplifying happened when a security guard reacted angrily to a teacher who, purposely satirizing a principal's directive that only emergencies qualified as reason to leave a classroom, called in an "emergency" request to the main office. The guard came running, followed by several others, only to hear the teacher, with a bit of a snide grin, say that a student only needed to go to the bathroom and that it "was an emergency." The security guard reacted angrily to the teacher in front of the students for creating such a furor, but then, as he walked down the hall, began rethinking his reaction. He immediately returned to the classroom.

"Excuse me for interrupting," he said, as he entered, "I just wanted to apologize for my unprofessional behavior. I let my emotions get the better of me. I don't think I was wrong for being upset, but I do think I was wrong for the way I handled it." To his credit the teacher not only accepted the apology but also apologized himself for engaging in such a thoughtless action. They shook hands, and left the students, it seems to me, with a powerful example of how to resolve a conflict. Not a bad lesson to learn, that not every fight has to be a fight to the finish.

SEVEN
Exercises and Outcomes II
Application

> Superbly good teachers become that way not so much because of a native ability, or even training, but because of a passionate commitment to teaching. —D. Cecil Clark

The key teacher behaviors outlined in the previous chapter define, in essence, *relationship behaviors*. How we behave in and out of the classroom by exemplifying, employing transparency, being empathic, and the like, are all really important to building trusting relationships and engaging students in the difficult work of developing positive habits. But, as was stated before, these, without well-formulated, well-planned, well-executed lessons, are simply not enough.

How we behave as human beings is critical, but how we behave as "professionals" (and in a broad sense this applies to parenting as well as teaching) is equally critical. As professionals, or as thoughtful parents, we need to have a purposefulness to what we do that focuses not only on inputs but on outcomes as well. Teachers especially, but really any and all of us, simply get more from our professional lives, and from our personal lives, when we apply intentionality.

Intentionality, in a way, is what Thoreau spoke of as when he wrote in *Walden*: "I went into the woods because I wanted to live deliberately." In the general flow of life you might say intentionality is just the habit of applying thought *before* action: in the shared language of this book you might call it having a *vision* before *initiating action*.

What I do I choose to do because I believe it will produce these specific results and, in respect of the direction I want to go in, this seems the best option. Not only is this our action, by the way, but it is also exemplifying: applying in our actions exactly those skills we want to infuse in our students.

As professional educators, intentionality is simply the understanding that in the end what we will produce in our students is by and large a result of what we plan in our lessons and in our interactions, and what we execute in practice.

We expect this, minimally, from almost every single professional with whom we interact. Before you would invest dime one, my guess is that you want to be sure that your financial advisor is not only an engaging personality, and capable of being attentive to your needs, but also exceptionally well versed in financial markets. Being a nice person alone will not ensure your stable and secure retirement.

Similarly, what we expect from a professional teacher, and from ourselves, is that we are exceptionally clear about what is expected in both the academic and the affective realms and, moreover, we can explain and effect what must be done to get each child there. The current climate that screams for longer school days and longer years and fewer opportunities for fun through the day wants these same outcomes but seems to be based on a teaching philosophy, long outmoded, that seems to imply that if it is fun, it is not learning. It seems also built on an immutable concept that however we used to do school in the last century is exactly how we should do school now, only, *because these kids today are "defective," we just need to do it harder.*

So far, it does not appear that this philosophy has actually yielded much in the way of growing the ability of our students to succeed on the personal or the academic level. Perhaps educator Albert Cullum was right when he opined: "We must remember how children learn rather than how we teach. Through movement, through emotions, through activities, through projects—all the basics fit in. And they're learning without realizing they're learning."

As thoughtful, meaningful actors, we need to develop intentions (and some quality control) as to what "product" our labors will produce and that we are producing what we intend. This does not preclude the lightning bolt of inspiration, though most often these better moments are built on well-planned foundations. Moments of spontaneity can be extraordinary, but a truly dedicated professional, measuring actual success in such a teachable moment, will certainly assess how such a moment was made to occur and turn the *inspiration* that works on occasion into *intention* that works regularly and with consistency.

Being professional at anything implies the ability to repeat with measured consistency an action, or series of actions, at a consistently high level of performance. One need not look much further than Yankee shortstop Derek Jeter to see a very public example of consistent professional excellence to which, though few achieve, virtually all baseball players aspire.

Information about his practice habits, gathered through the public media, seem to indicate that Jeter's excellence is an exercise in preparation and planning. Although to be sure we have seen the dynamic and sudden brilliance in his many spontaneous dramatic moments, it is the focused repetition of certain actions and habits that has woven for him this fabric of regularly solid, even superb, performance, on which he can embroider an occasional moment of splendor.

In truth, extraordinary teaching moments can occur with amazing regularity in classrooms even where the planning is spare. Often, even in these circumstances, many teachers are able to seize the moment and make powerful, even transcendent teaching choices that lead to thoughtful, meaningful, and, perhaps most importantly, pedagogically sound outcomes. However, because of this lack of planning, even potentially great teachers let these moments slip by with responses that miss the mark of effectiveness or simply devolve into personal digressions that may excite the teacher, and even the students, but impact little on any objective.

However, if in learning and teaching victory is accomplished "step by step, not by leaps and bounds" (as it was for pioneering auto racer Lyn St. James, as it is just about everywhere else), then consistent effort sweetened with these transcendent moments is our aim. The question then becomes not how often such moments happen, or even how brilliantly they are capitalized on, but rather how often such moments can be created, with the same level of effectiveness, as planned activities in structured, outcome-driven lessons.

DENSE LEARNING: USING PLANNING AND LEARNING TIME EFFECTIVELY AND THOROUGHLY

> The harder you work in the classroom, the less they learn. —Carol Lefelt, master teacher

Indifferent, ineffective lessons are more usually the lack of intense planning and preparation than lack of great teaching potential: Cecil Clark might call it a lack of a "passionate commitment to teaching." This is especially important when the learning is something, such as success skills, that require long periods of practice and reflection.

There is no way around the fact that the kind of preparedness that frees one's mind from having to think through the fundamentals while still being mindfully in the moment to search for the potential that may be unfolding does take commitment. As was mentioned before, Aristotle reminds us that "we are what we repeatedly do. Excellence, therefore, is a habit, not an action."

However, because of the critical importance of teachers in respect of student achievement, there has been a tendency to make teachers responsible for everything. Because of that, in developing practices for exceptionally dedicated and busy teachers, it is also critical to be acutely aware of all that is already on the swollen list of regular teacher expectations.

While the instructional value of much of what teachers are being asked to do may be debatable—some certainly has great merit—what often gets asked for is so consistently time consuming that it gets done half-heartedly, if at all. Even teachers whose dedication is admirable speak frequently, and accurately, of being overwhelmed.

The good news is that infusing both critical thinking and critical skill development into lessons rich with knowledge growth need not demand more teaching or planning time than is currently required (though, at the outset, like any new process, it may take additional time to get up to "speed"). Best of all is while planning is streamlined, the learning created is rigorous.

All that is required of teachers in order to increase teaching effectiveness and learning rigor is that they plan a little differently in order to use classroom time differently. To increase teaching effectiveness and learning rigor we only need to combine a layer of behavioral learning and critical thinking in the same learning period that has been typically fact or information based.

The form "Steps to Writing Effective Lesson Plans" has been adapted from a critical-thinking-skill lesson-development organizer created by Dr. Walter Cmielewski and others in the Education Department at Caldwell College in New Jersey. While functional proficiency using this lesson-plan development tool is relatively easy to master, it may take a bit longer to apply it with consistency in a deeply developmental way. However, once accustomed to this format it becomes no more difficult to develop and employ a lesson plan rich in critical thinking, a core element of rigor, as it does to create a less challenging lesson.

Moreover, the relationship between developing critical thinking skills and developing success skills cannot be underestimated. Imagine a student capable of making sound, long-term life decisions, and you will be imagining someone who, at least on some level, has developed a modicum of proficiency in at least some critical-thinking skills.

Exercises and Outcomes II 109

Steps		
1. Identify the topic for the class: _____ Select a critical success strategy: (How is the strategy to be infused into the lesson or class structure? ? (Combine with critical thinking strategy when appropriate)	*Critical Success Strategies/Skills* Persistence Self-Regulation Interpersonal Skills Time Management Organization Decision Making ***Individual Practice*** or ***Whole Class Practice*** *working lists for personal practice* *single strategies all work on at once*	
2. Select the **critical thinking** for the student learning objective.	**Critical Thinking Strategies** Problem Solving Decision Making Information Processing Concept Formation **Critical Thinking Skills** Sequencing Cause/Effect Distinguishing Fact/Opinion Identifying Relationships Predicting Comparison/Contrast Distinguishing Reality/Fantasy Recognizing Patterns Classifying Detecting Bias Drawing Conclusions Summarizing Categorizing Identifying Logical Fallacies Making Inferences Establishing Criteria	
3. Ask: "What do I want the students to be able to do to show that learning is taking place?" 4. Ask: "What are the conditions under which this objective will take place?" "After reading the chapter…" "While completing an essay…" "Given a set of …"	**Student Learning/Behavior Verbs** 	Knowledge	Comprehension	Application	Analysis	Synthesis	Evaluation
---	---	---	---	---	---
List	Explain	Apply	Categorize	Create	Justify
Recognize	Expand	Organize	Compare	Predict	Appraise
Describe	Demonstrate	Group	Contrast	Design	Judge
Match	Summarize	Relate	Analyze	Infer	Criticism
Identify	Paraphrase	Classify	Examine	Compose	Prove
Name	Calculate	Utilize	Deduce	Change	Evaluate
Recite	Define	Solve	Dissect	Construct	Decide
Outline	Understand	Manipulate	Simplify	Generate	Rate
Locate	Report	Illustrate	Scrutinize	Combine	Weigh
Find	Retell	Initiate	Inspect	Formulate	Determine
Select	Cite	Show	Uncover	Invent	Prioritize
Record	Review	Develop	Conclude	Originate	Convince		
5. Ask: "What will the students actually be doing?"	**Lesson Activities** | Student Centered	Teacher Directed
---	---
Think/Pair/Share Role-Playing	Lecture
Panel Discussion Project Work	Teacher Reading Story
Numbered Heads Together Jigsaw	Teacher Lead Discussion
Completing Graphic Organizers Research			
6. Ask: "What are the assessments which will measure that the objective(s) have been met?"		**Formative**	**Summative**
---	---
Homework Reading/Writing Workshop	Performance Assessment Essay
Journal Writing Observing Students	Writing
Logs Running Records, Facilitation	Assignment Portfolios
Grids	Multiple Choice, True/False, Fill-in (tests)	

Figure 7.1. Steps to Writing Effective "Dense" Lesson Plans

For a general overview of how to apply this organizer, assume you are an American history teacher readying a lesson for students to be able to identify several major events that led to the American Civil War. Any simple, basic lesson plan ought to be able to answer at least three basic questions to be functional. These are *the big three*:

1. How is a student going to be smarter when they leave than when they arrived?
2. How will the activities help them become smarter in the way intended?
3. How in the hell will we know if they are, or are not, smarter?

A *rational* answer to the big three above should satisfy any supervisor that the teacher, at least, came into the classroom prepared to be effective but, as with any profession, teachers must make a personal choice as to what level they are going to aspire. Effective teachers do manage to have careers that are effective, and that is fine. But high-impact teachers have memorable careers. If you have made the decision to both have *and exemplify* the deep level of commitment that excellence requires, being able to answer the big three is just the beginning.

Here is a lesson objective that, essentially, meets the requirements of the big three:

> Students will be able to identify, and recite, six major events that led to the American Civil War.

At the end of this lesson the students will know the six events, they will learn it through the activity of committing it to memory, and the teacher will know who has learned it by listening to their recitation.

Memorization has its value, to be sure, and in this instance it may well be important to be able to be highly familiar with the sequence of events that took our country to a powerful conflagration. However, regardless of the importance of knowing these events, this is a low-rigor lesson irrespective of how many facts the teacher drives into the students' gray matter.

Yet, those same facts being weighed for their causative connections, *while being memorized*, actually ask students to apply a higher level of rigor simply because they are being asked to deduce a cause-and-effect relationship, a critical-thinking skill. So we move from a memorization objective to student action that extends the same learning in a more complex way:

> Students will be able to identify six major events that led to the American Civil War and be able to put them into an order of importance and commit them to memory in sequential order.

BOOM: *instant rigor!*

In the *Understanding by Design* construct, which this organizer was developed partly to embrace, critical thinking must be planned into the lesson as a clear and measurable learning objective, just as surely as being able to remember said fact acquisition must be planned into the lesson as a measurable objective of each student's learning. In fact, the critical-thinking manipulation of these facts can actually be the very engine that drives their memorability.

The entire act of learning becomes, in effect, a single confluent action of several strands of interconnected learning (that can be assessed individually) rather than a series of sequential learning activities learned separately over the same period of time. This is step one in creating the structure for *dense learning*.

Typically, lessons tend to focus on one or two things at time under the theory that the more that you have going on the less likely you are to be able to get kids to pay attention and learn. While this may be true when it comes to the "width" of the lesson (i.e., the information, facts, events, and even skills that must be learned separately or sequentially), it may not be true when talking about the lesson's "depth" (how the information is acquired, used, etc.). The reality is that some kind of learning skill must be applied during the lesson anyway but, left only to students to determine, they are likely to find the least resistant path by relying on comfortable, familiar approaches: rote memorization rather than causative analysis.

In this history lesson example, the opportunity to employ a critical-thinking skill deepens the objective by integrating a more rigorous, complex process to a rather straightforward learning aim. Deepening lessons—that is, adding another well-planned developmental layer—should not take significantly more class time. Additionally, because skills are always adaptable to developmental levels, lessons are easily differentiated to maintain a level of difficulty appropriate for each student. Therefore, adding a well-integrated, critical-thinking skill layer can increase rigor without significantly adding time, ease differentiation, and add significant long-term value to the learning.

In this Civil War lesson students are now applying a critical-thinking skill to capture knowledge. In order to accomplish this, the teacher has added a research component where students validate facts and establish a hierarchy of importance. However, in many schools access to resources is often limited and problematic. At best, most classrooms have a handful of working computers, so having whole-class time for anything technological is an issue.

However, by thinking of critical success skill development as an additional lesson component, we can overcome limited resources and foster a success skill at the same time. Assuming this teacher is just starting to foster independent learning skills, the teacher might want to find a means to begin to get students accustomed to self-directed responsibility. The teacher has decided to set up research-skills development stations where one group can engage in learning how to determine cause and effect, another is identifying great internet resources, a third group is reviewing books and taking notes, and one group is on the computers doing research. The nature of such stations can reflect the needs of the learning, but the key is to create a structure that serves both the learning and the development of success skills.

Normally, when it comes to centers, teachers often create and manage the rotations. However, if students plan and manage their own schedules, organizing, planning, managing, and utilizing time effectively become uniquely integrated into the learning. Scheduling software, freely available on the internet (e.g., Google calendar), collaborative planning docs, or just old-fashioned paper and pen will help students manage their own schedules as well as keep the teacher able to both track and facilitate student progress.

To employ learning densely, it is critical to be able to be comfortable with having several moving parts going at the same time. However, the guided-planning-process organizer is designed to simply and effectively develop clear student expectations in all areas of a particular lesson. These can be supported by clearly written, qualitative rubrics that define student learning expectations. When objectives are clearly and accurately defined, managing and assessing multiple student learning strands becomes that much easier. Planning this way also assures that skills and content, not activities, are what is central to the lesson. Education author Nancy Sulla calls it assuring "brains-on," rather than hands-on, learning activities.

So, where the average classroom learns dates and facts, the excellent classroom adds critical-thinking standards into the learning. The superior classroom infuses into that same time period the learning of content, critical-thinking skills, and success skills as well. Best of all, where subject-specific information is not always transportable to other areas of learning, success and critical-thinking skills always are transferable.

Imagine, if you will, that you are in a school where the majority of everyone's class time is initially focused on these transferable skills, as it was in Maryland's *Tools of the Mind* classrooms. Initially training in self-regulation absorbed a high percentage of class time, but in short order these transferable skills, thinking ahead and regulating behavior, became a part of the structure. You might say they started carrying around these skills in their backpacks, along with their other learning materials, like their pencils and notebooks.

Eventually the students in the *Tools of the Mind* classes started having much more rapid academic growth than a like class run in a more traditional way, though, at the outset, the traditional class progressed at a faster pace. More importantly, just like Mischel's "Candy Kids," the *Tools of the Mind* students have tended to outperform their classmates who have had more traditional school experiences all throughout their academic careers.

These critical skills, infused into the lessons we teach and through our interactions, go a fair bit toward creating the magic of dense learning and using time effectively. In the same space of time where one thing was accomplished, now several things are being taught. Rigor, planned diligence, and the ardor for learning are all wrapped in the package of a lesson.

Learning, after all, rarely just falls into our heads. To be sure it can be driven into our heads, like a nail, with misery and pain, but rarely, if ever, does it fall. Want proof? Walk into any academically accelerated class being taught by a stern task master and just watch.

SUCCESS SKILLS IN THE TECHNOLOGY AGE

> I have witnessed many technological changes in my lifetime, but none have done away with the need to learn ethics and develop character in the individual. —Bernard Baruch (1947)

While technology has eased some of teacher responsibilities and made quicker work of such tasks as revision, as Ruth Schwartz Cowan wryly observed in her essay "Less Work for Mother," "time-saving" inventions such as vacuum cleaners and washing machines did more to remove the work from household workers and make it the responsibilities of the homemaker than it did to make free time.

Similarly, technology has also ended up placing more work in the purview of teachers and line administrators than it has reduced their workload. In part this is because more is being asked of remaining individuals as technology and shrinking budgets have reduced the size of school staffs. It is also because technology is either misused or used in a less efficacious way than it could be used.

Lesson plans, for instance, are essentially not written any faster on a computer than they are on a notebook page, and if the use of them ended there, it wouldn't matter. However, increasingly plans and such have become part of the record-keeping required of teachers, and printing and collating sixteen tons of plans and data to meet the requirements of federal and state oversight committees has made them burdensome in ways that have been unexpected.

However, if lesson plans are constructed on an interconnected cloud-based system, such as Google Apps (full disclosure: I refer mostly to Google Apps for Education because as a certified trainer, I am most familiar with these tools. This may not be a better system than others, such Sharepoint, Office360, and iCloud Apps, which may work equally well, or better, and are also available for little or no cost), would allow teachers to both control the level of privacy and still have the ability to make the plans widely available with a few clicks. That would make administrative access instantly available and decrease the time-consuming nature of collating them for the purpose of internal or external evaluation as well as data management.

Moreover, digitized documents created or residing on common could-based systems allows for easy editing and sharing and can be accessed from any internet-connected computer anywhere in the world. Documents that have to be sent, or physically taken from one place to another, can now be instantly shared for professional purposes, curricular development, communication, for creating an online lesson-plan library, a learning-reminder system, a how-to library, or even a self-directed study system that can foster independent student learning and increase positive, proactive, and pro-learning home-school communication.

While technology is inconsequential in developing character and habits central to critical success skills, technology does play a huge role in the need for such skills in the lives of our students. So where and when possible, facilitating, training, informing, and guiding done through technology reaps added value and additional benefits. The modern, digital world has made information readily available through MOOCs, on-demand learning sites like Khan Academy, blog sites, wikis, and even Wikipedia (to name a bare few) and has engendered a significant shift in the role of educators. Where once teachers delivered "new information" with the expectation of validity, now information is available everywhere and teachers must train students to assess the accuracy and validity of what used to be vetted for them.

For these reasons, infusing technology into the learning of these skills (as well as for communication and management) is very important. For a closer look at how this can occur, let's shift back to our history classroom, and to the learning we are doing regarding the run up to the Civil War.

The lesson, essentially, asked students to be conversant with a series of events that led to the Civil War. Some class time was dedicated to this but, as with most classrooms, the increasing demand to cover wider swaths of curriculum, and meet the learning needs of diverse learners, makes using only dedicated class time highly unlikely. However, through technology we can make it possible to continue the learning beyond the bell without increasing the already-considerable demand placed on teachers.

Successful differentiating lies not solely in the teacher creating and assigning different work to students but rather in allowing students to discover and travel multiple paths to the same objective. In so doing the teacher continues guiding and facilitating, but it is the student who develops not only the ability to define and understand his *learning machinery* but also develops personal responsibility for his or her own learning, an important success skill trait. Since in a well-constructed lesson plan, activities, readings, and resources will be already identified, why not continue to employ such already-completed work to augment teaching?

A class/teacher website, simply and easily constructed, can actually become a classroom extension allowing lesson plans and resources to extend the school day. Technology commonly in use (e.g., Smart-tech or other presentational technologies) now allows teachers to create and/or record instruction and make it available online with little extra effort.

One immediate effect of pre-recording a lesson is that it allows a savvy teacher to clone himself or herself. The recorded lesson, especially when such a lesson necessitates proximity to the front board for instructive display, frees the teacher to be both the instructor in front of the room as well as a co-teacher circulating among the students assessing and facilitating. A facilitating teacher is more likely to be able to interact around academic and success skill development in a way that allows students to internalize behaviors. More powerfully still, an assignment posted on a website, linked to the recording of the lesson, doubles the power of the teaching in as much as the same lesson can be reused at the students' will for review and relearning.

Essentially a recorded lesson (and even the lesson plan and resources that are a part of it) becomes, in the oft-used advertising phrase, *the gift that keeps on giving*. In respect of teaching a student self-reliance and other critical skills, it affords immediate and unlimited review, allowing the learner who needs more time and repetition an amount of time sufficient to meet his or her needs. It also offers students who have missed a class, or new students entering the class, an opportunity to review lessons conducted in their absence to get or stay current. Lastly, students who may want or need additional review for projects and testing have the resource at their fingertips as each lesson simply becomes another in a series of "how-tos" available whenever and wherever it is needed or wanted.

Thus a lesson outlining the difference between nouns and pronouns and proper nouns becomes, on another occasion, with no additional work for the teacher that created it, a "just-in-time" learning experience for any number of students from that class or even from other classes. This "gift" for the students also becomes a gift for the teacher, as it frees him or her from the responsibility of being the only knowledge repository of the lessons and activities of the class.

But wait, there's more!

Even apart from the service it provides to the students in their quest for independence and for the teachers in their quest to help students become motivated, responsible, and self-regulated learners, the posting of lessons adds even more value. When lessons, assignments, learning links, how-tos, and so forth are posted online, they become a means for teachers to track their own work and for supervisors to stay abreast of teacher progress. Additionally, it also becomes embedded, positive, ongoing, and regular professional communication with colleagues, and, especially, with parents. Frequent and positive home communication augments our ability to create a "familial" school that seamlessly connects learning from home to school and from school to home.

Most professionals understand and value such communication but, for a myriad of reasons, chief among which is time, are unable to sustain such communication long term. Hence a huge percentage of communication between school and home (the figure has been pegged as high as 90 percent) often winds up being negative simply because the time element makes only those most pressing issues, such as a student's disruptive behaviors in class, rise to the level of crisis worth the sacrifice of time.

What most parents seem to want to know teachers are already keeping accurate records of anyway and would willingly share, were there enough hours in the day. However, to serve the basic information needs of the vast majority of parents, the technology is simple and probably already in use by the school. While employing class websites to open a window into what students are learning, we can also use technology to securely share information on the academic and affective progress of their child and what they can do to support that learning and growth.

This kind of on-demand communication, which is leveraging work already done, still reflects positively on the school and on the teacher. It also enhances the personal and professional communication that effectively supports the "clinical" model that would most effectively support the common purpose of teaching success skills.

Record-keeping, tracking progress, and sharing information is simplified in a digital environment by using spreadsheet tools, forms, communication, and data-management software. For instance, if Sally's teacher, as we discussed before, makes an informed decision not to enforce consequences for a particular infraction, why not? However, her ability to record said break and have it appear immediately in a shared record gives another teacher wrestling with a similar decision the ability to know almost immediately if Sally has been skirting her responsibilities. Instead of cutting Sally another "break," the conversation changes, quite quickly, to a discussion that begins with an immediate "what's going on?" Research has been uniformly clear that the more quickly we are involved in corrective behavior or with interaction that may result in student self-correction, the more effective and meaningful it will be.

And if that weren't enough, whoever is mentoring Sally in our "power of ten" structure, Sally's counselors and parents or guardians all get this information immediately. Want to discuss it? Want a meeting? No problem! Multiple people can view this data at the same time in remote locations (assuming internet access) and communicate all without having to leave the place where they happen to be. Most teachers, administrators, and parents would be more than happy to contribute to a meeting that affects the well-being of one of their students. Being able to do so in a way that has minimal impact on their ability to conduct a personal life makes all that much easier to do.

Often the meeting is not the problem but rather the three or four extra hours of having to be onsite waiting or having to commute back to a physical site that forces a choice between being an engaged professional and an engaged parent that creates the real conflict. Want to have an online meeting at 7:30? Not a problem. Want to do some collaborative curriculum planning after the kids are asleep at 9:30? We can do that. Time and information-sharing problem solved! There is much technology that can be adapted to enhance the effective practice of managing schools and school communication and in helping students develop the kinds of skills that enhance not just their learning today but their ability to continue to learn and grow.

MOVE A LITTLE, MOVE A LITTLE, MOVE A LITTLE MORE

As mentioned earlier, *in success skills, the product is the process*. Especially because it is a process that rarely produces a clearly predicable outcome, assessment can be complicated. Yet assessment is a critical a component of teaching and learning and absolutely informs us, as professionals, how effective we are. "Student learning," as noted earlier from educator Mel Riddile, "is not about the student's ability to learn. It is about our ability to teach them."

In most cases assessment is most effective when drawn from an amalgam of measurements, data, and observations, sometimes even collected over long periods of time (the effects of learning are sometimes revealed at a considerable distance from its receipt). This is especially true of a highly process-oriented program like learning critical success skills where increments of learning, traditional measures in testing, are not always revealed until a need for their application presents itself. Most of us can easily recall in a moment of crisis being visited by a message from the past similar to the example of the student story shared in the preface.

Parents, of course, have the greatest opportunity to develop and observe these kinds of dialogue-centered relationships that facilitate both practical and conceptual self-knowledge. But teachers, too, have time to help students explore their inner lives and still meet curriculum requirements, pacing guides, and administrative edicts. As noted previously, it is a matter of using time effectively.

While measuring our professional effectiveness is always critical and necessary, we must also be mindful that assessing individual progress in behaviors of any sort can be complex and in need of constant adjustments so that we can constantly redefine how we teach and what we should be expecting as a result. Just to be clear, using these data-management techniques is not absolutely necessary to ensure successfully teaching these skills. As Eliot Eisner, a leading educational reformer, has said: "The more we stress only what we can measure in school, the more we need to remember that not everything that is measurable matters, and not everything that matters is measurable."

However, using data to make behavioral and instructional decisions can be a critical component of many well-managed classrooms and schools, if it is used properly and well. In assessing a process-oriented program that involves changing human behavior, attention must be paid to *thought* as well as to action. While assessment in our data-driven instructional culture does not always value intention, sometimes understanding, even if it has not yet become consistently infused into the dynamic of action, can be an important critical marker. A simple reality alluded to earlier is that, ultimately, there can be no intentional change without first the thought of change. Of course, even when that thought has been formulated into action, the path forward is rarely smooth.

Responses such as this one, by a high school faculty member, reveal a total lack of understanding of the process of change, or at the very least, a lack of desire to deal with it. She gleefully noted that a student's recent progress was a complete sham because, after a few days of moving in a better direction, he had engaged in a negative behavior similar to those he had been engaging in previously. "Looks like your big project with [name of the student] is a failure," she happily declared.

Since with this program we are empowering our children (and perhaps even, on occasion, ourselves) to make and follow through on purposeful life decisions, respecting the ambiguity of the thought process and managing the frequently chaotic struggle are paramount. Although the old adage "money talks" indicates that only final results matter, in our construct thought and intention also talk.

Strategies and actions that could become positive change are born in "the will to become the best that you can become," said Canadian legislator Harold Taylor. Yet as complex as it is to measure will, persistence, and intention in our assessment of progress, not doing so opens a door to self-delusion. "The easiest thing of all is to deceive one's self," notes the ancient Greek philosopher Demosthenes, "for what a man wishes he generally believes to be true."

Running records, the ongoing reading-assessment coding system, provides at least a clue to how complex activities (in this case reading) can measure definable progress in multifaceted skill development. In applying the concept of running records into a means to assess progress in success skills, we would need only to define specific behaviors that are components of a complex activity, such as persistence, and to try to be attentive to these components as well as the overall "fluency" of a whole skill application.

The complexity of the range of human thought and activity can certainly make this a much more daunting task than assessing reading, a comparatively slightly simpler endeavor. However, by staying focused on the key behaviors, one can track progress that might reasonably be connected to improvement in the particular success skill identified. Here is an example of some behaviors that, taken together, identify progress toward mastering each skill.

Persistence
- Time on task
- Managing frustration through self-regulation
- Assignment completion

Organization
- Able to identify required tasks on an ongoing basis
- Is able to prioritize importance and level of urgency of each task
- Has a clear picture of what time, resources, and tools are required for each task

Time management
- Uses existing or has created a means by which a schedule can be monitored
- Employs a clear strategy for time use that is built around individualized best times
- Understands using time for both efficiency and excellence

Interpersonal/Social Skills
- Uses self-regulation to decrease reactivity to stimuli
- Is able to use a sense of humor appropriately to ameliorate internal/external tensions
- Conforms to appropriate norms for the situation including dress, language, and attitudes

Decision Making
- Has a clear and specific outcome goal in mind for "important" decisions

- Is willing to take the time to fully explore alternatives when possible
- Is always reflective before, after, and during decisions and makes adjustments accordingly

Self-Regulation

- Is able to define personal needs and have a clear sense of purpose (short and long term)
- Is goal oriented and thinks ahead to define impact of choices on the outcome of goals
- Is process oriented and breaks down complex tasks into multiple, achievable steps

These are suggestions, and not intended to be inclusive of every possible behavior that underscores each of these complex and multifaceted skills. There are infinite ways to adapt this structure to embrace differing needs and perceptions of these elements. The key is to create unified agreement on what these elements are and to create ways to assess, rather than assume, student progress in respect to internalizing complex behaviors. Table 7.1 shows an example of a very simplified way, using the running records format, that can also be set up as an interactive, efficient cloud-based system to track student progress.

Table 7.1.

behavior	how taught	spoken	acted upon	assessment	follow-up
persistence	personal discussion and goal setting in respect of homework	identified desire to increase grade, created a homework plan (over a period of two days) to complete seven missing homeworks	completed 1 homework and stopped	spoke of being overwhelmed but even so managed the first. It took such a long time that she imagined the impossibility of completing all the work and so quit.	Discussed the idea of re-planning to provide more time to complete task. . . .

In keeping with the idea that we are attempting to create a "clinical" model, or community of collaboration, having useful, accessible information freely shared among involved parties is critical. Less relevant is whether it is observationally or quantifiably collected. As we refine the community of discourse and develop this "common language" noted earlier, students as well as professionals will develop this unified familiarity, which can foster more accurate and clear communication not only of student learning but also regarding what inputs fostered this learning so that we're not constantly covering the same ground unnecessarily.

Equally critical is to engage the students in measuring their own progress toward their stated short- and long-term goals. In the end, of course, *this skills-based process has to be, primarily, about the student's journey to self-efficacy.*

Again, this complexity does not easily lend itself to traditional assessments that plot clear progressions on a trajectory toward a specific learning outcome. What may be considered the right choice or the wrong choice, for instance, is of little use in such assessments. Discovering what you don't want is every bit as important as finding out what you do want.

Helping students reach concepts of self-definition, and to master skills and positive attitudes, is more like shopping for clothing. We often have to try on one garment and then try on another and sometimes try on that first garment again, in different sizes and colors, until we find not just what fits right but what also looks right and feels right. And even then, as most of us have learned through actual experience, sometimes what looks and even feels right in the store winds up not being exactly quite like we remembered it by the time we get home.

How a teacher builds this into the classroom experience is made more complicated by assessment and data tracking needed to fulfill professional responsibilities in the results-oriented classroom. At the same time, such information is also central to the student to build the necessary personal responsibility to define goals and internalize skills.

Employing the system explained above as a means to self-assess progress makes such a measure more critical than if it were used purely as teacher assessment alone. The added advantage, of course, is that transparently and confidentially shared among the team, it becomes yet another source of information for savvy, collaborative teachers and other school personnel that can be used to help the student continue to recognize his or her own power regarding personal achievement.

However, please note that all "internal" or professional communication need not be equally shared. Reiterating an earlier explanation, transparency is not necessarily sharing everything and anything. Rather, using "back channel"–type communication judiciously among parents and professionals, which often lacks clarity and has nuances of thought that might be misconstrued by less-nuanced thinking, can sometimes be more harmful then helpful when shared.

It is perfectly appropriate to choose what is shared among adults and what ought not to be shared with youngsters, and every "clinical team" needs to develop principles that guide what is appropriate for their students and circumstances. Of course, since building student trust is a critical key, teams should choose to be transparent about what information is collected and shared without necessarily sharing the specific information.

Likewise, in certain circumstances, students may be comfortable sharing something with an individual yet, knowing the reporting practices, may choose to have that specific information held close. Remembering that open communication among responsible parties limits the power of manipulative behaviors, having policies under which such action is appropriate, and when it is not, will help assure confidentiality without disrupting the necessary sharing of information.

Lastly, creating and using self-guiding assessments refers back to an earlier concept of employing some kind of affirmational structure. The (even quasi-) public expression of the starting of a journey, of writing it down even for your eyes alone, has an undertone of commitment and therefore enormous power. Likewise, so does tracking progress toward that goal in a meaningful and positive way.

While public commitments, such as people make in marriage, or even commitments made in informal circumstances, may not always result in lifelong bonds, and they probably slow down relational entropy. We understand that even in the most committed relationship conflict will occur but, in taking the risk to go public, so to speak, we also challenge ourselves to resolve these conflicts as a matter of personal pride. A young teacher posted on the front wall of the classroom this quote attributed to Robert Schuller: "What would you attempt, if you knew you could not fail?"

The compelling reason to be public about our quests, with a genuine expression of a real and honest and deeply felt objective, is that the journey toward any objective is fraught with a myriad of opportunities to quit and thus to fail. Accomplishment, particularly *great* accomplishment, is as much an act of will as it is an act of talent or intelligence. "Let me tell you the secret that has led me to my goal," said scientist Louis Pasteur. "My strength lies solely in my tenacity." The public commitment (even if it is "public" only to oneself—that is said aloud or written down) is often a powerful motivator to see the job through.

Being successful, realizing your objectives, *is* hard work, and although some may find fortune by merely opening their doors (my father used to say that even a blind pig can find an acorn once in a while), teaching and learning critical success skills is about creating habits to foster success rather than merely living on the hope of finding success. The focus on that alone makes for as compelling a reason as one might need to speak aloud and powerfully that which we want to achieve.

However, equally complex is the journey itself and the adjustments that are so much a part of the struggle. Filmmaker George Lucas observed that "part of the issue of achievement is to be able to set realistic goals, but that's one of the hardest things to do because you don't always know exactly where you're going, and you shouldn't."

Any assessment that drives this kind of process-focused activity needs to be more of a beacon of illumination rather than some kind of locked-in homing device. In all of our personal journeys, destinations can and should be changeable, but carefully: changed on the basis of changing desire, or changing circumstances, or just simply because when you got "there" it wasn't quite what you expected so it's on to another dream. "Never stop because you are afraid," warns explorer Fridtjof Nansen. "You are never so likely to be wrong." We have to accept that in learning some of the greatest moments of discovery are not narrated by the cry of *Eureka!*, but rather are accompanied by the epithet *Crap!*

Great discoveries are sometimes these difficult moments and can leave us with wisdom that would not have been acquired any other way besides taking a chance, totally screwing the pooch, but having acquired learning from the experience. No less a scientist than Charles Darwin said, "I love fools' experiments. I am always making them."

When our children hit the wall, as we all sometimes hit the wall, it is infinitely more important to have information from you as their teacher, as well as others, how we, too, from time to time have hit the wall and had to struggle to put all the pieces back together. Believe absolutely, this is not the moment when they need to hear self-aggrandizing boasting about perfect scores whether true or untrue.

What students do not need is a trusted adult to demean their efforts or to tell them what they *think* the student *must* do. What students want, what most of us want, is not the answers that have worked for others, but rather how someone exemplified in a crisis how the habits helped them restore equilibrium or even how they exhibited a measure of hope and courage in the face of overwhelming despair so that they could just keep on.

What students need is a compassionate person who will just patiently listen as they begin to talk through and take the first tentative steps back onto the road to success. What students need is not an answer but the time and the guidance that lets *them* ferret out for *themselves* what they need to move ahead. What students need is to evolve their own usable process that they can apply and reapply to help themselves in this moment, and help themselves forever.

Afterword

What Matters Tomorrow Is Tomorrow: Closing Thoughts

Decisions do define us, but we are made whole by the experiences and learning we get as a result of those decisions. While not every decision has meaning, each moment of learning matters, no matter how many billions of them we have throughout our lives, even when they come at the expense of a few or even a copious amount of tears. Poet John Berryman said that "a writer should feel very grateful indeed to have been put through an ordeal that does not actually kill him."

The writer's art is fueled by just such experiences, just such learning, and so are our lives.

Whether writer or not, learning even through misfortune can add great value to one's life. Notes the iconic singer Pete Seeger, "Education is when you read the fine print; experience is what you get when you don't." It's learning either way.

The moving findings of a study tracking a group of Norwegian high school students related high school struggles to later success. This study found that those students who went through hardships and somehow prevailed (whether academic, social, or emotional) developed greater resiliency and, most importantly, a set of skills that equipped them to deal with life's ups and downs. Though as a group they were not necessarily wealthier or more accomplished than their peers who had an easier time in high school, they were generally happier and more content with their lives.

This is not to say that bad is ever good. People can learn through positive experiences just as well as they can learn through those that are negative. The example referred to earlier about a child being publicly and mistakenly identified by his third-grade teacher as "retarded" may well have motivated that child to excel, but it in no way ennobles the outright cruelty of the teacher's comments. More to the point is a comment by Bernard Malamud, who wrote about the difficult lives of grocers and baseball players and writers and matchmakers. About suffering Malamud said, "I'm against it, but when it occurs, why waste the experience?"

Our students operate in two time zones, only one of which is in school. In the *school zone* we watch our students struggle, and often feel deeply for them. Their issues sometimes seem alarmingly simple to fix from our perspective. Our maturity and experience, our ability to see more clearly, makes us think, *If only he would. . . . If only she would. . . . If only*. In reality, fixing a problem is sometimes the right thing to do, and sometimes it is not, but it is always difficult to know which is which. However, for the most part, any day is just one day and any decision is just one decision of many decisions and days that flow in the *life zone*. Life is longer but school is sometimes more powerful. Our main effort, above all, is that as professional educators we ought to try to assure that what we do in school time does not damage the students' hope for change, and for a better future, in lifetime.

The purpose of this entire book is about being able to teach our children and our students, as best we can, a reasonable empowerment that respects the truth about where and how we can have control over the lives we live. It is a book about creating a platform of understanding as to what our students, our children, need to know in order to live lives that produce satisfaction, contentment, even true happiness whether they do or do not have all the material success that's featured on too many television shows.

Our children are starving for truth about how to bring meaning into their lives. They are also starving for meaningful guidance that does not hurt them or weaken them, but rather strengthens them, to make powerful, meaningful decisions on their own and to realize their true potential, which is the one they see for themselves, the one that they truly see for themselves.

Reiterating the earlier quote from Bertrand Russell: "It is because modern education is so seldom inspired by a great hope that it so seldom achieves great results. The wish to preserve the past rather than the hope of creating the future dominates the minds of those who control the teaching of the young."

This book was written to be the most incredible, powerful, game-changing, life-changing, and world-changing book about education that has even been written, or could ever hope to be written. But reality indicates that since no book that has come before it has been that, it is unlikely that this book will be any different. Perhaps the next book will.

In the absence of that, the intent of *The Missing Link*, whatever its flaws, is to contribute, even in some small, meaningful way, to the way we teach children these critical success skills. As educators, as parents, as people in the village responsible for the well-being of the children we all share, all we can ever hope to do is create the opportunity for our children to be able to develop the wisdom to find the opportunity in every challenge, the skills to maximize that opportunity, and the temerity and grit to succeed despite any forces that have happened to have gotten in their way. When we can effectively teach even a little of that, then we will have indeed helped create a hopeful future.

www.ingramcontent.com/pod-product-compliance
Lightning Source LLC
Chambersburg PA
CBHW052051300426
44117CB00012B/2075